TATTOO DESIGN BOOK

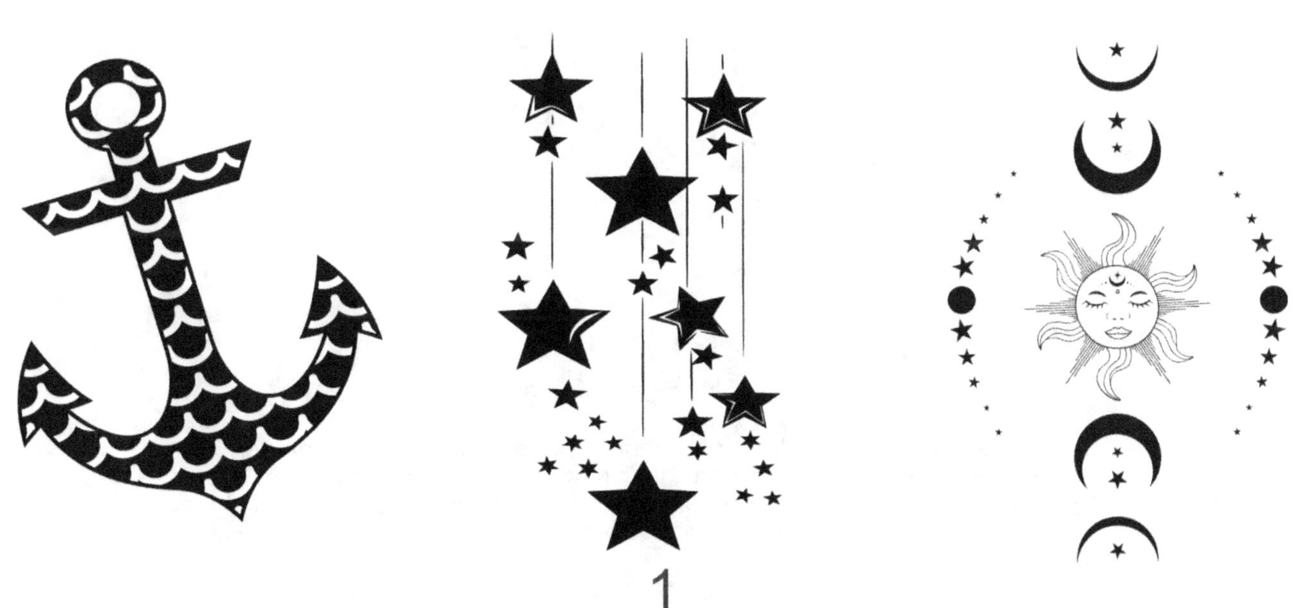

MINIMALIST ART TATTOOS

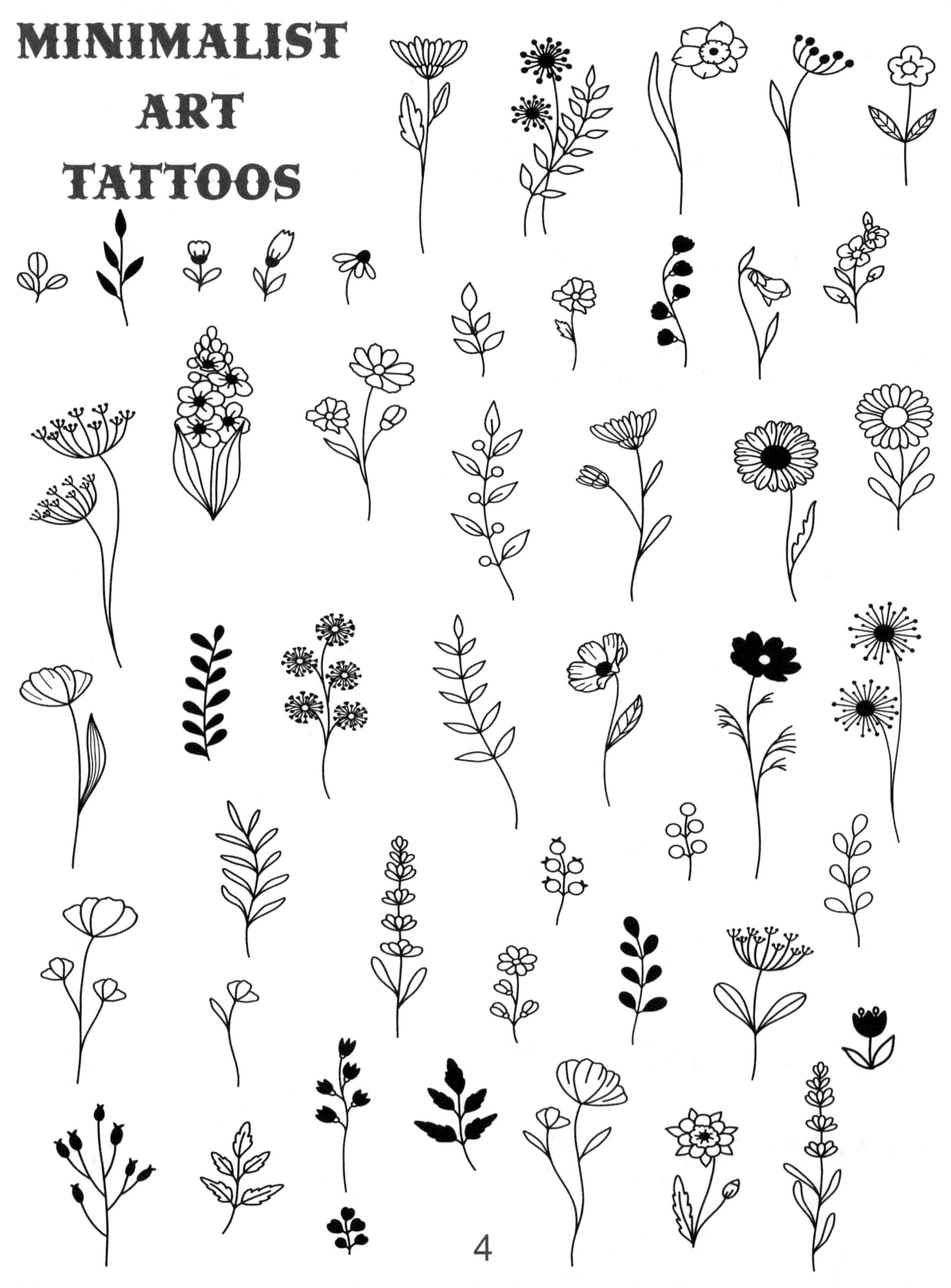

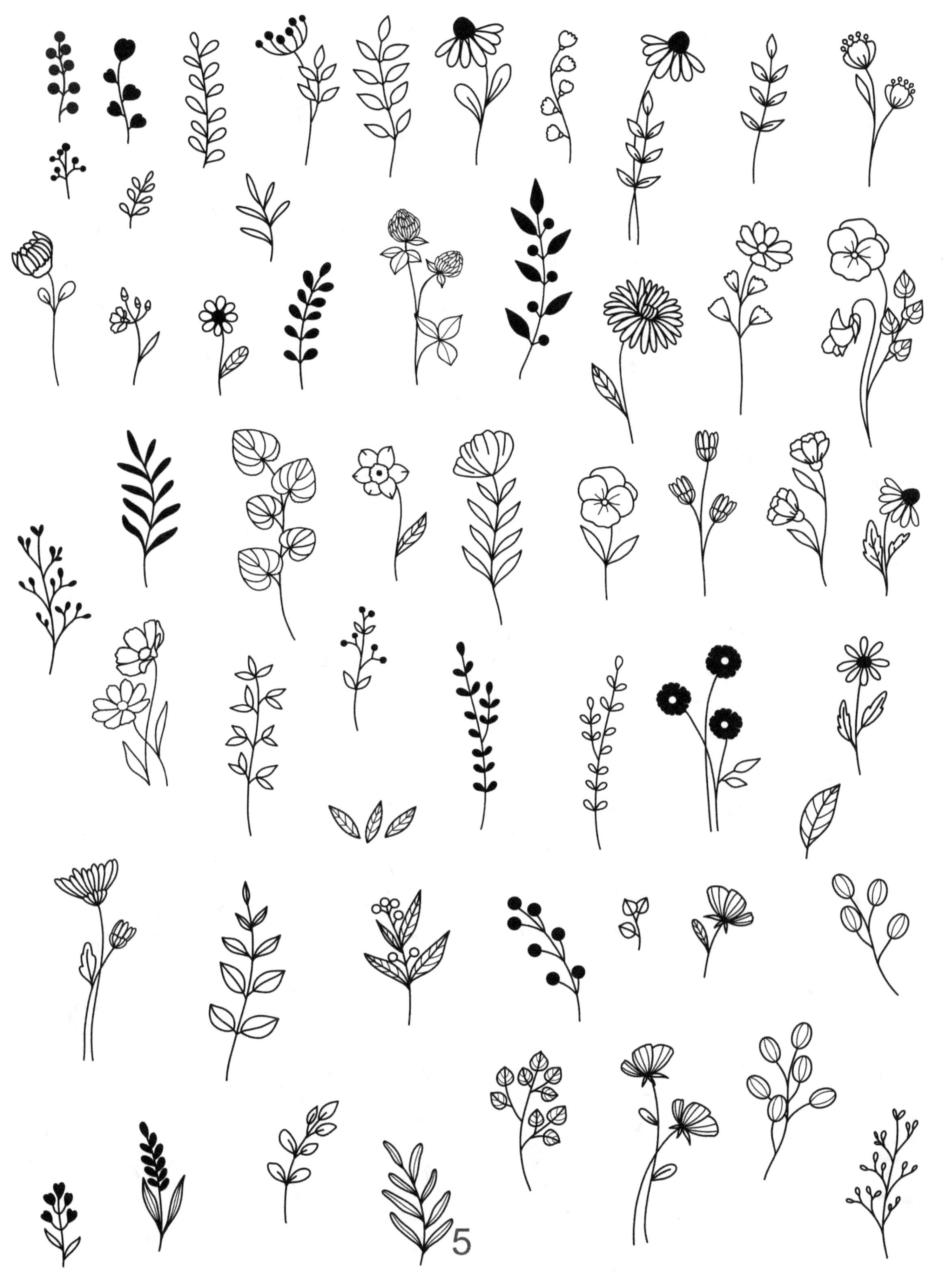

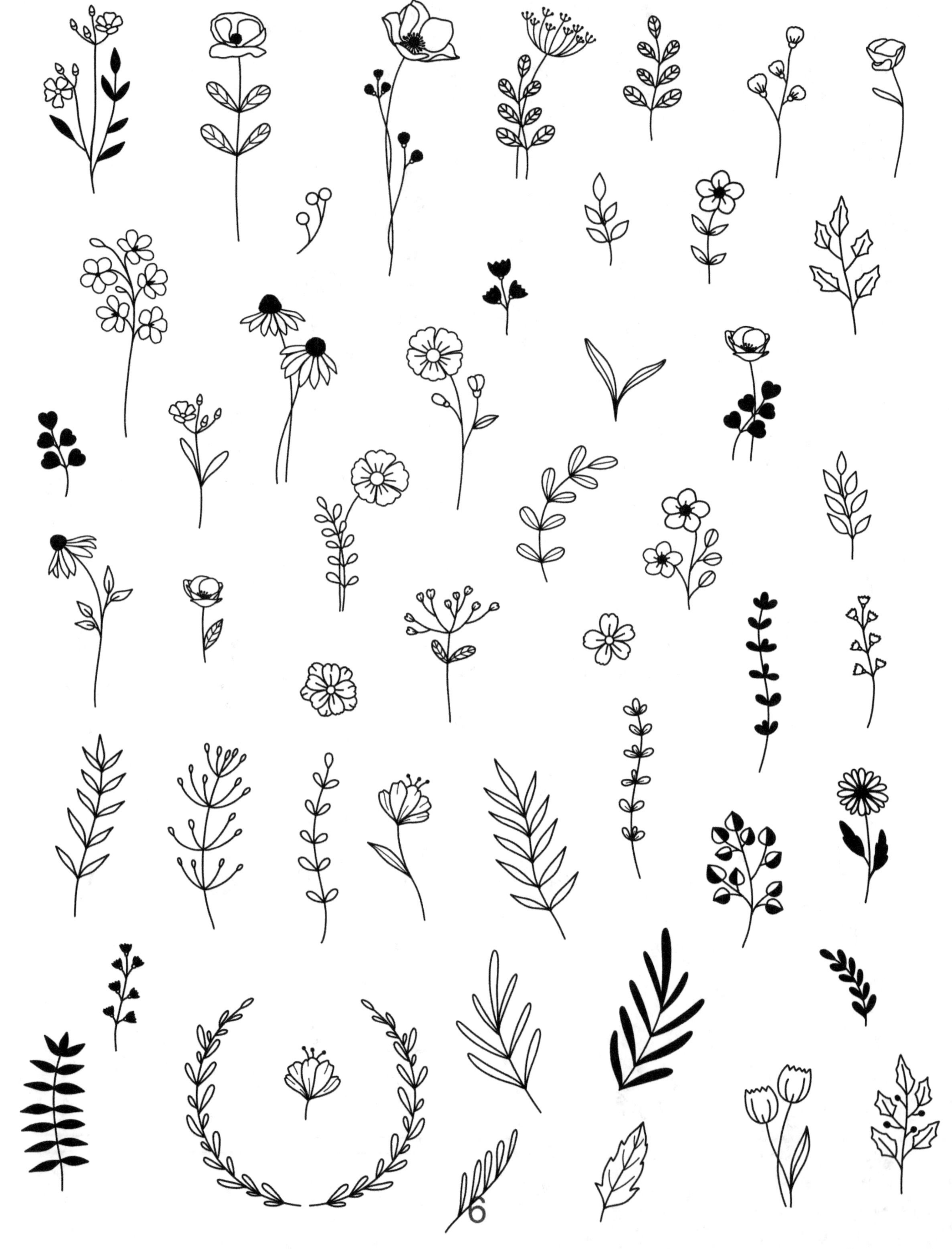

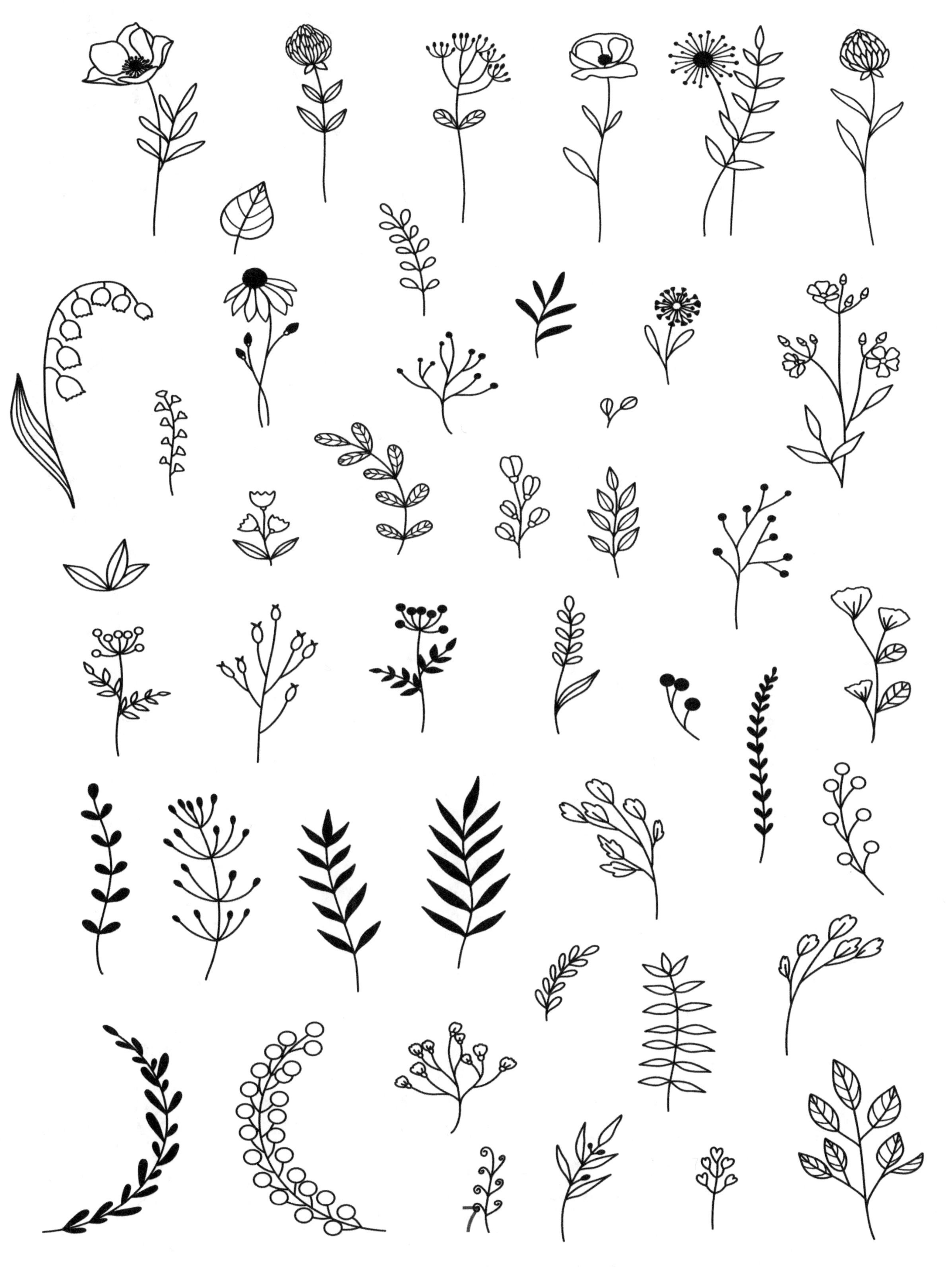

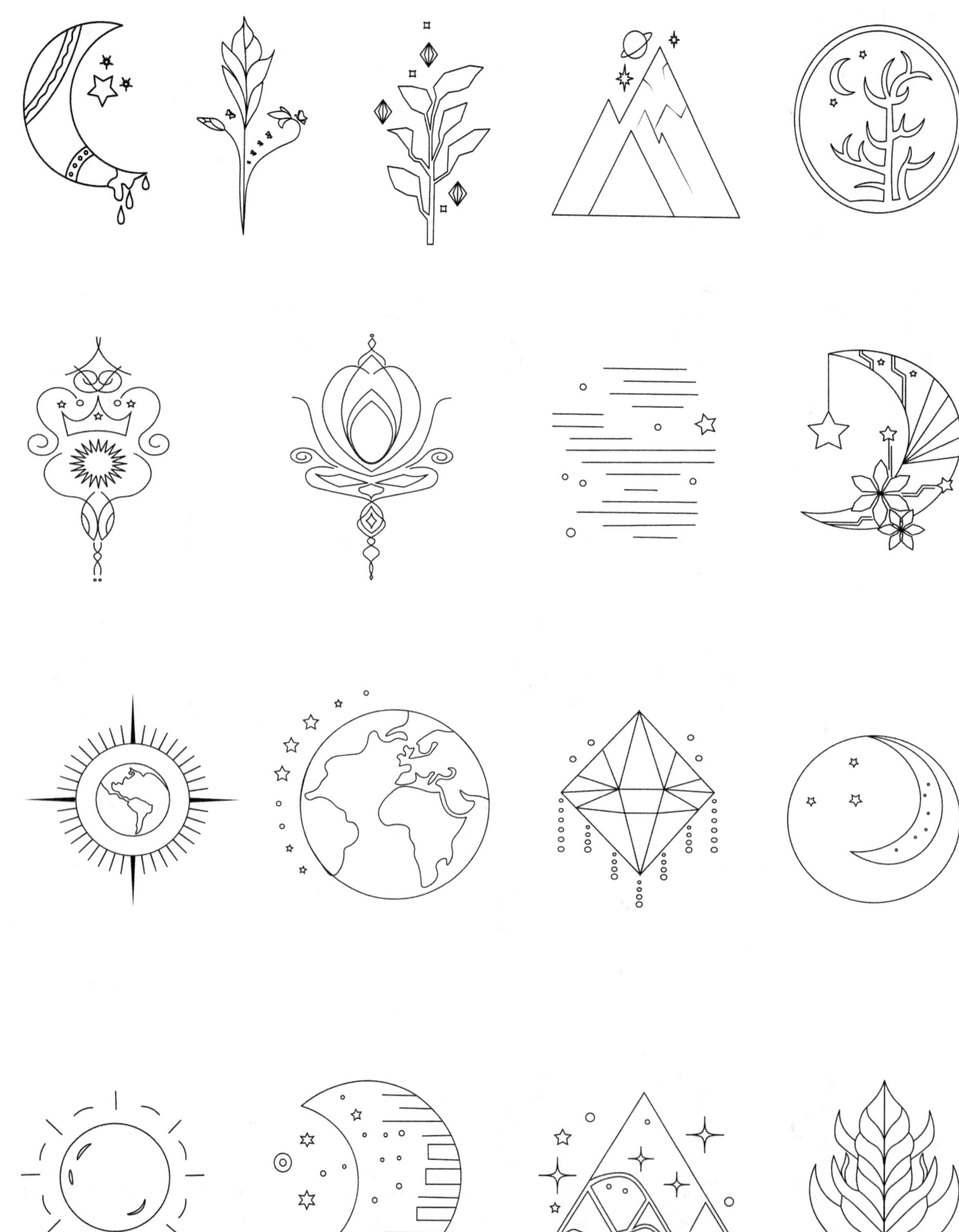

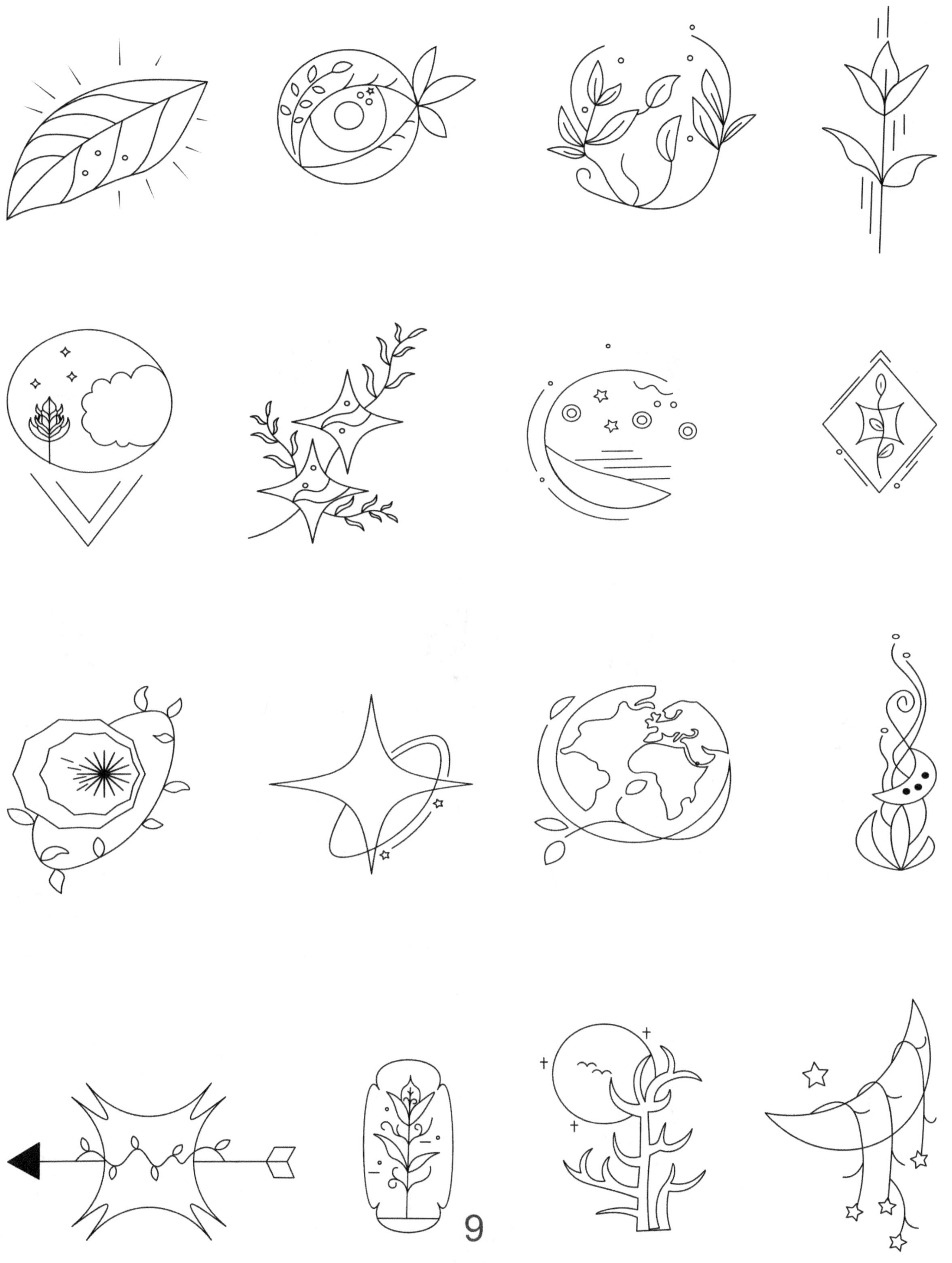

9

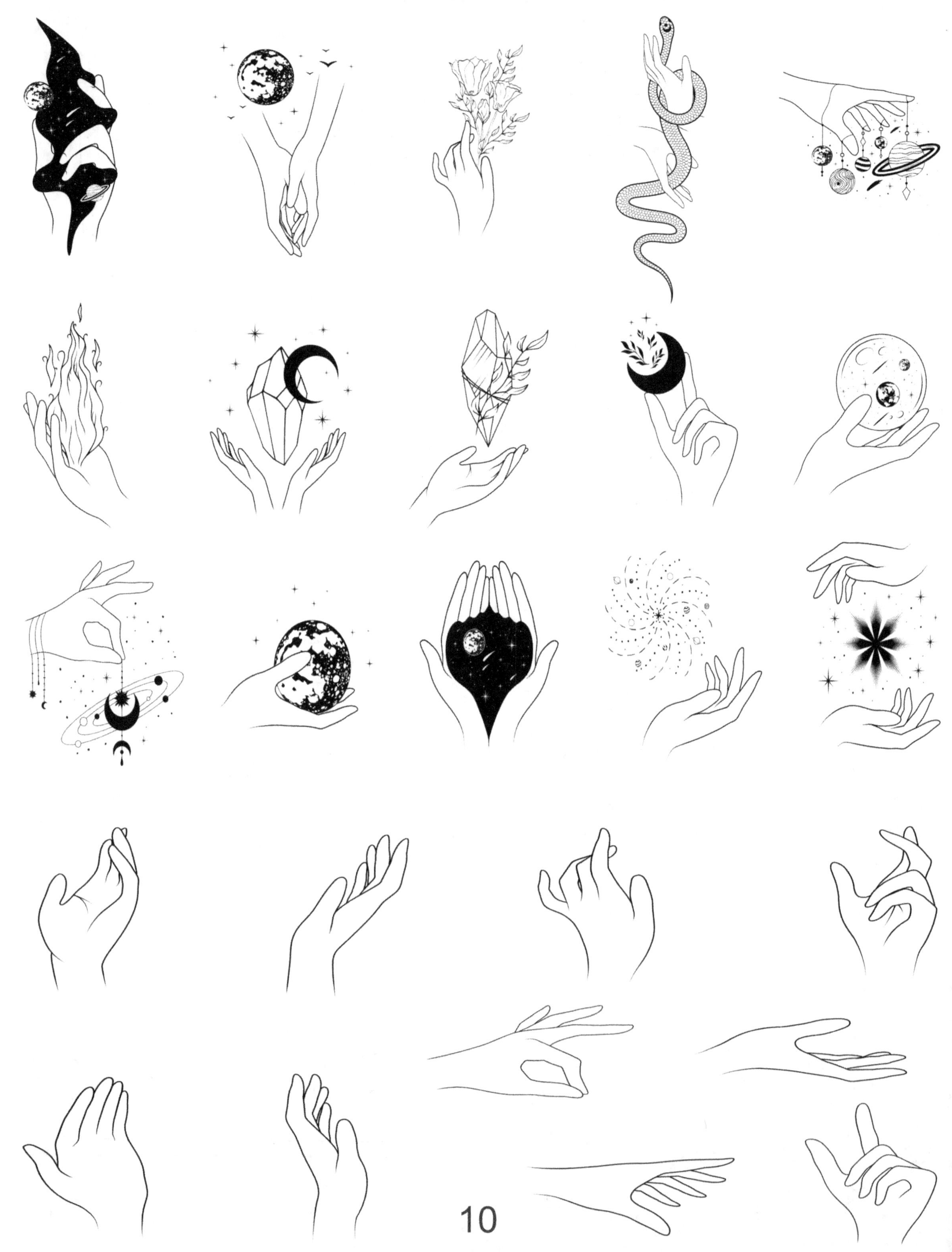

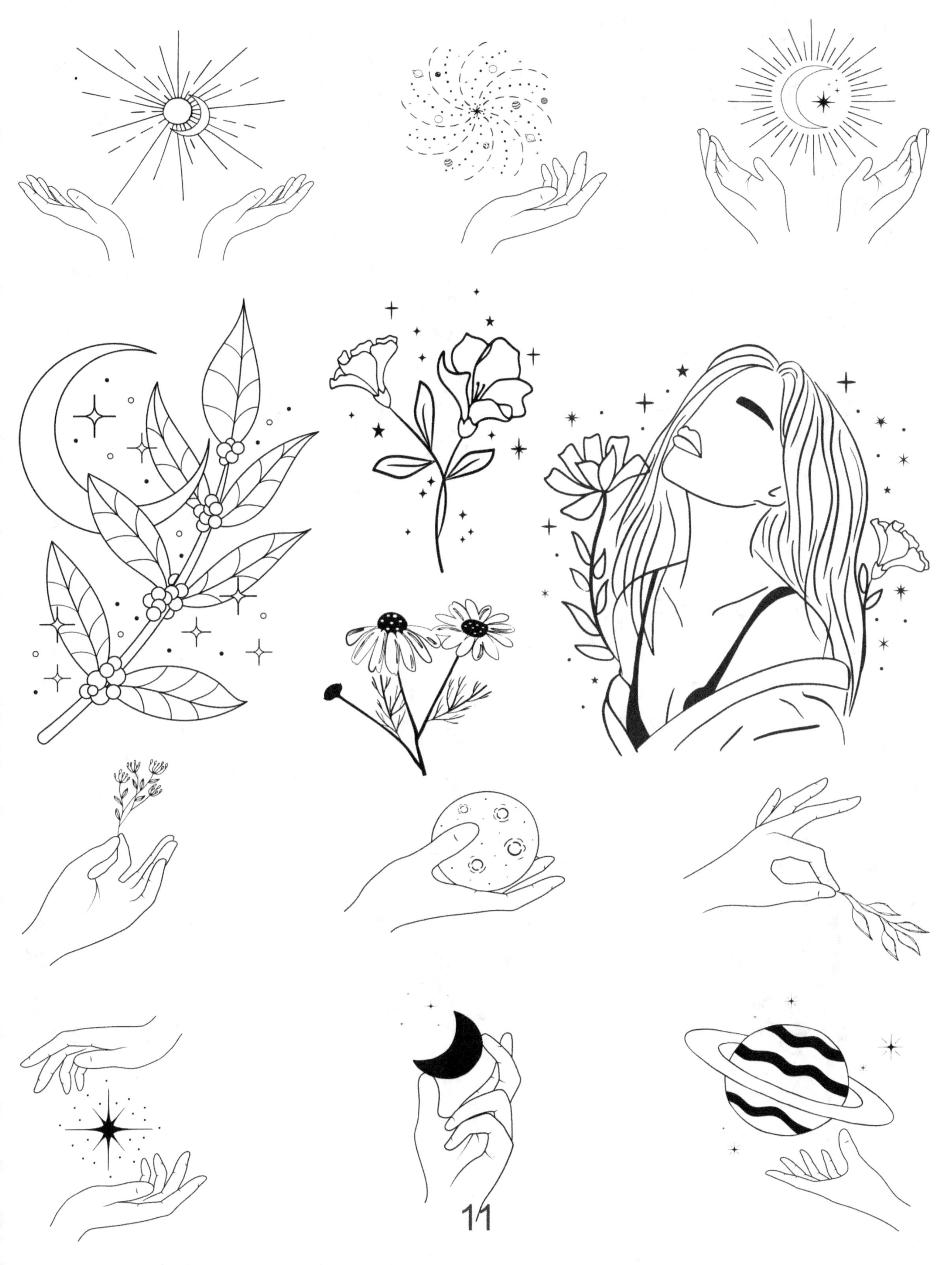

DREAM CATCHER TATTOOS

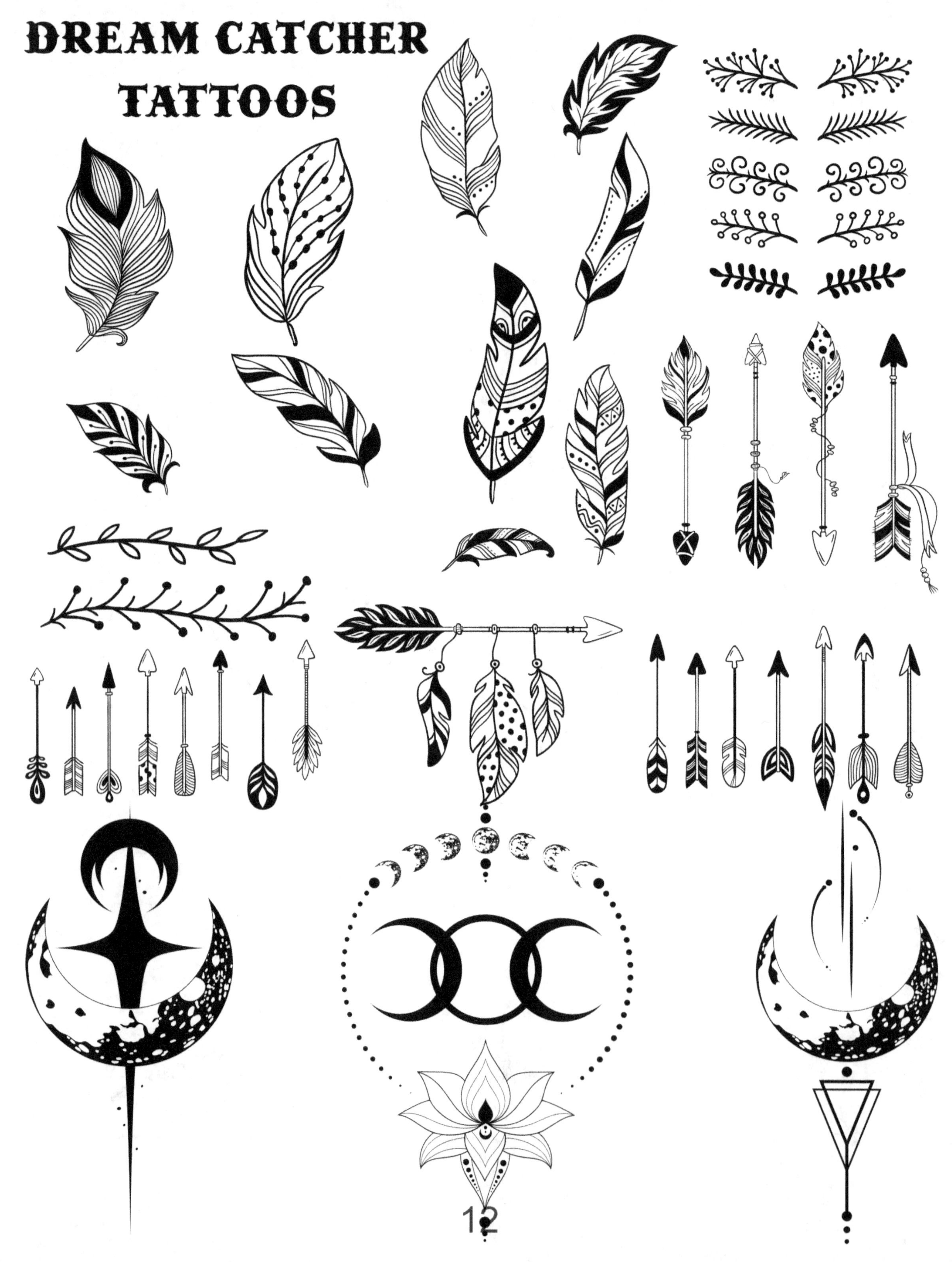

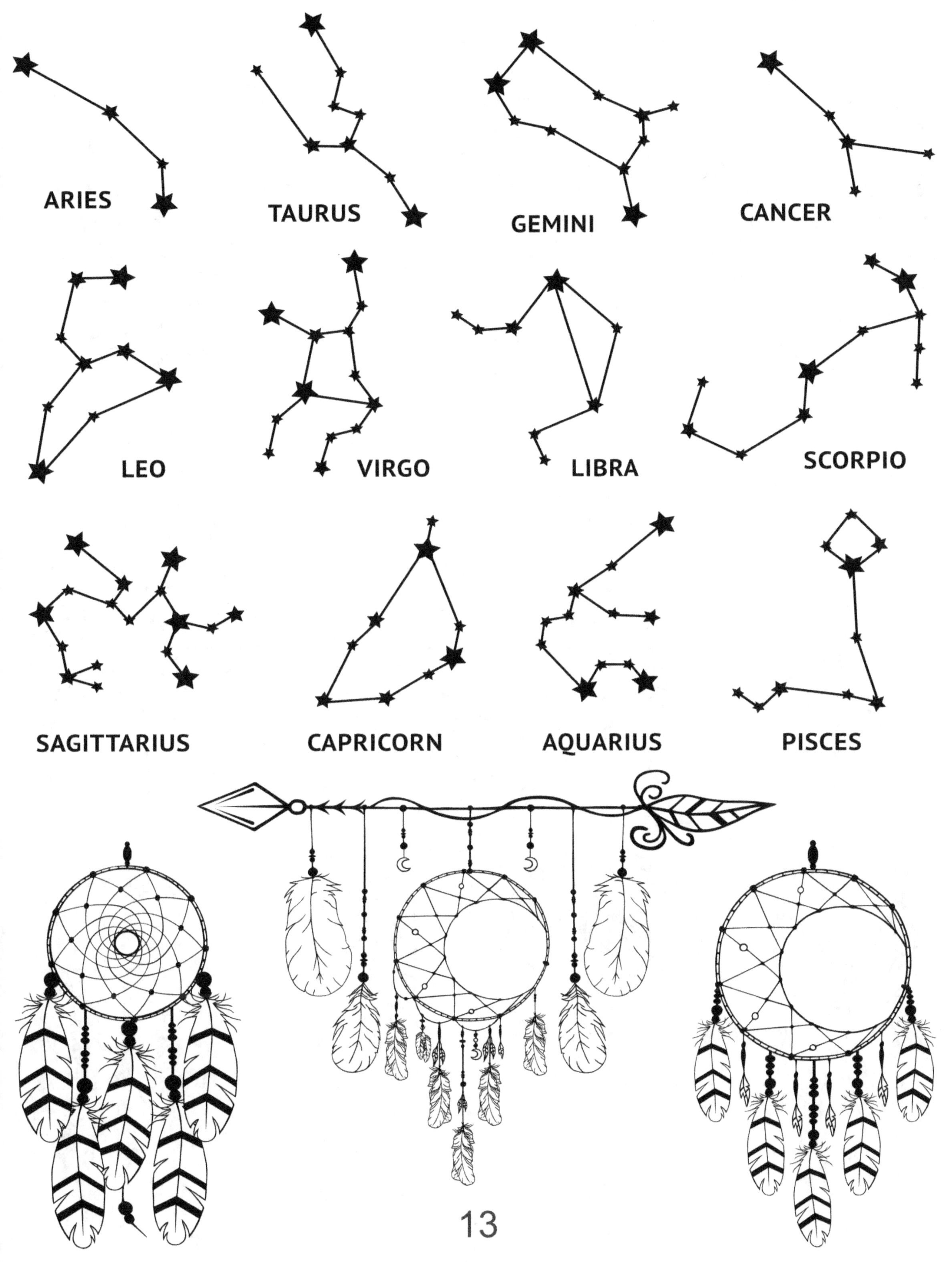

ARIES
TAURUS
GEMINI
CANCER
LEO
VIRGO
LIBRA
SCORPIO
SAGITTARIUS
CAPRICORN
AQUARIUS
PISCES

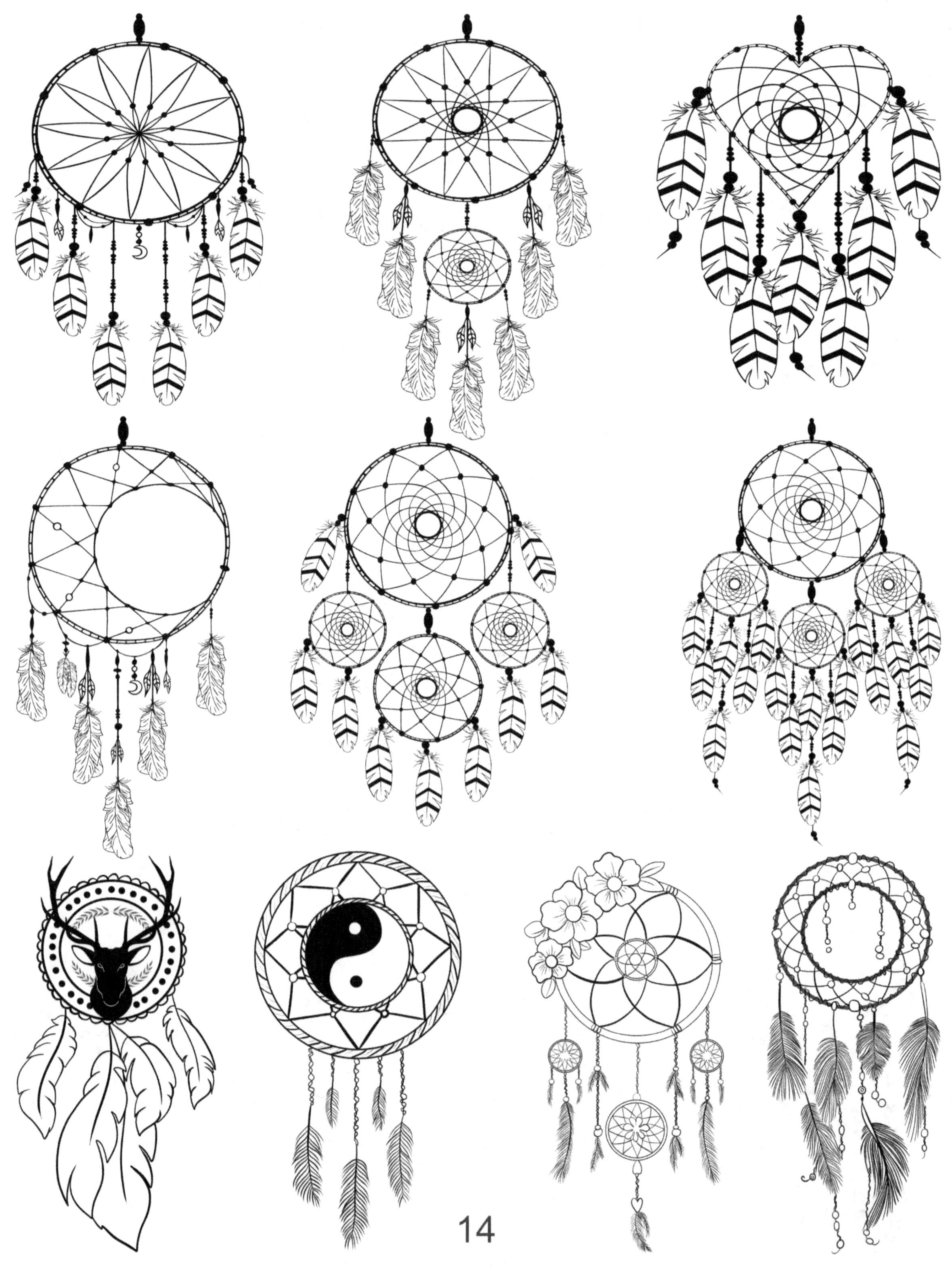

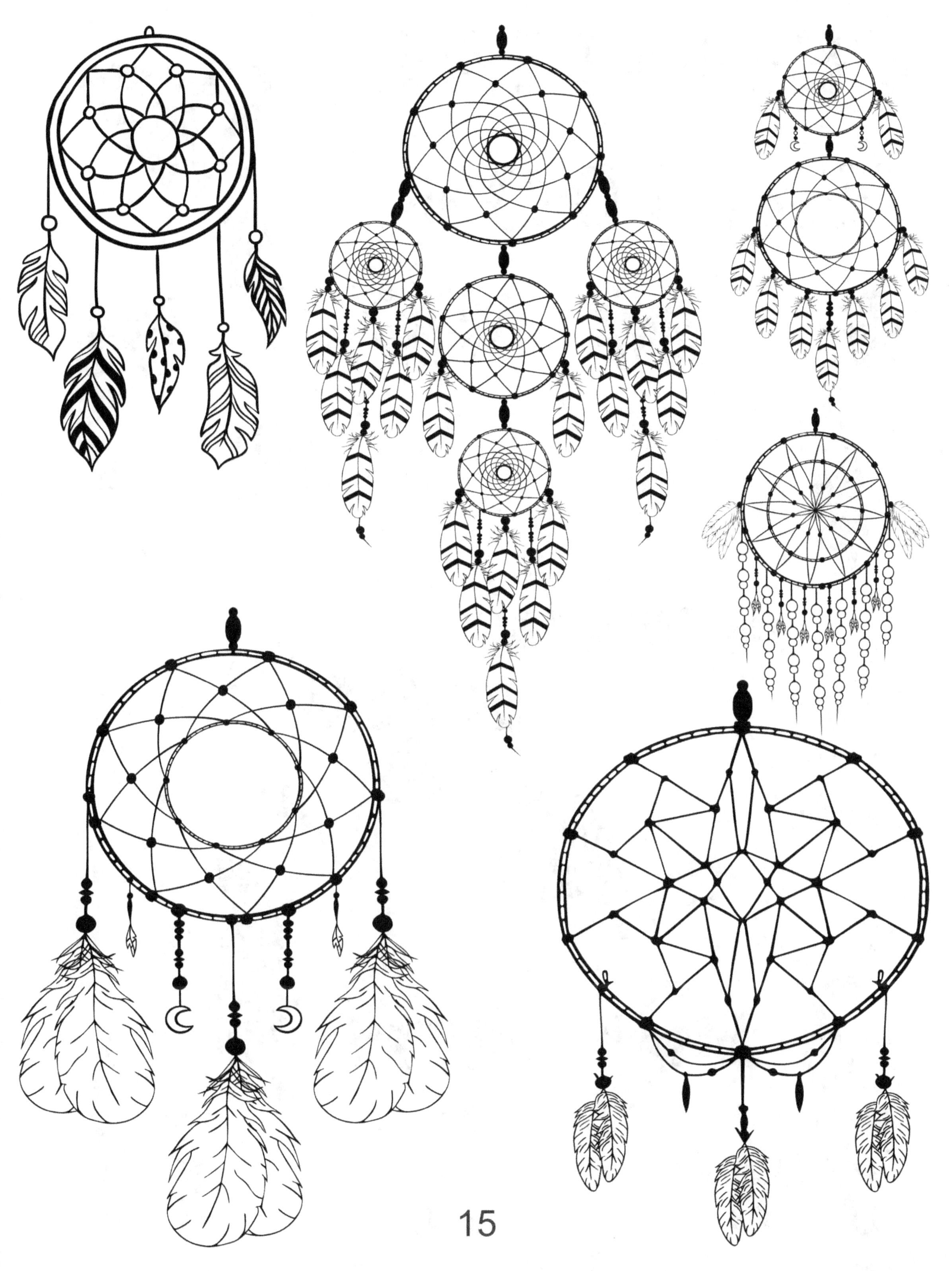

CELESTIAL TATTOOS

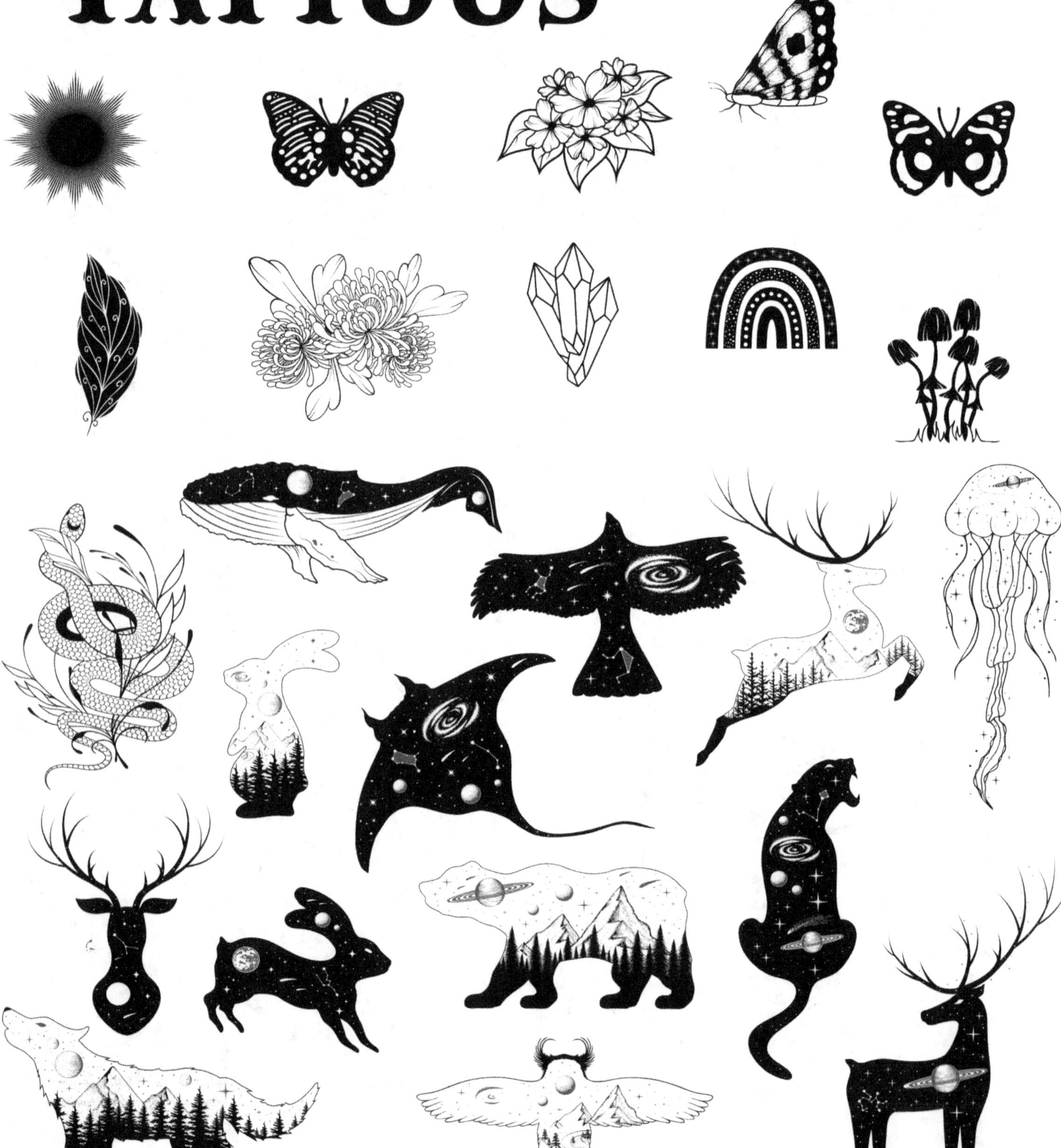

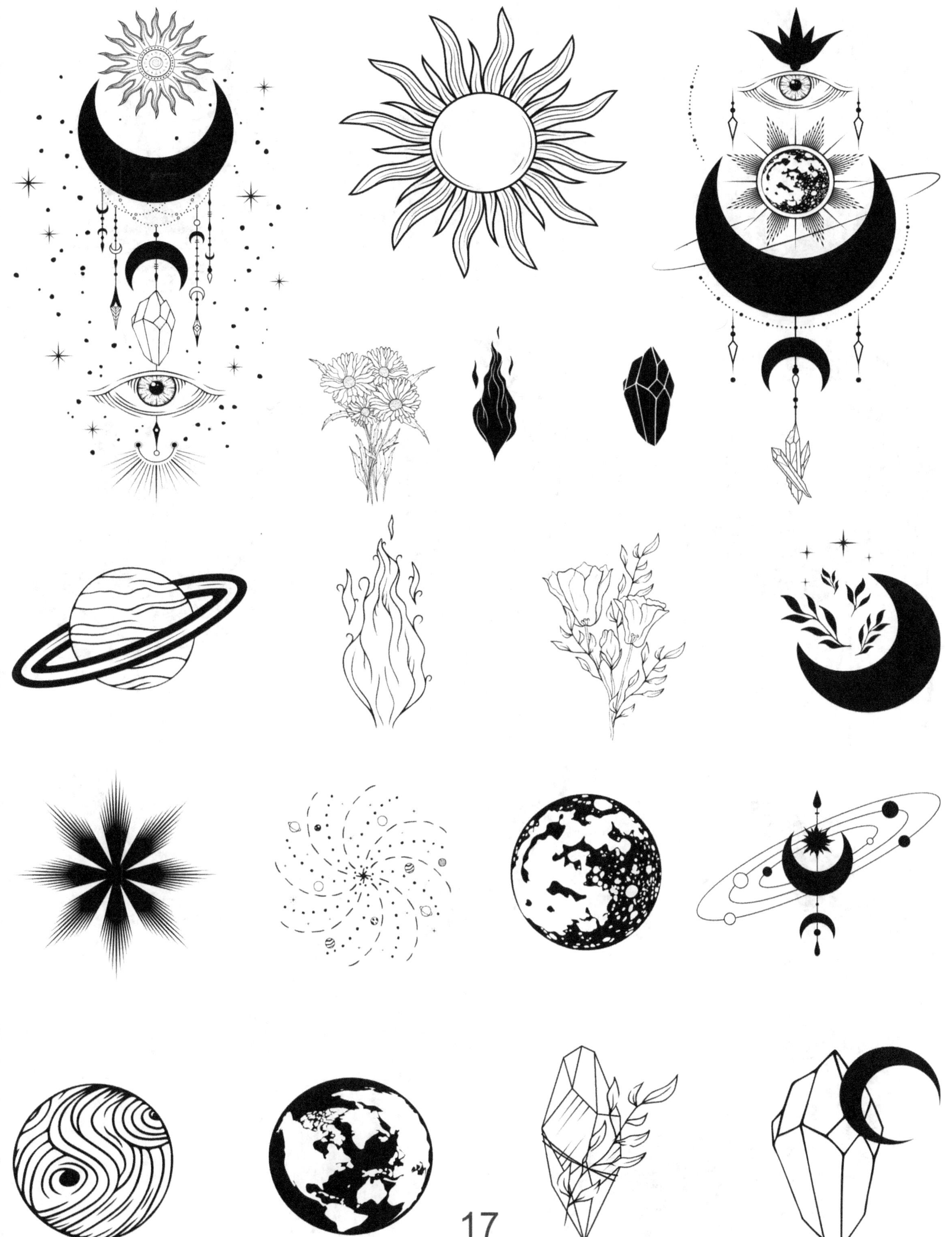

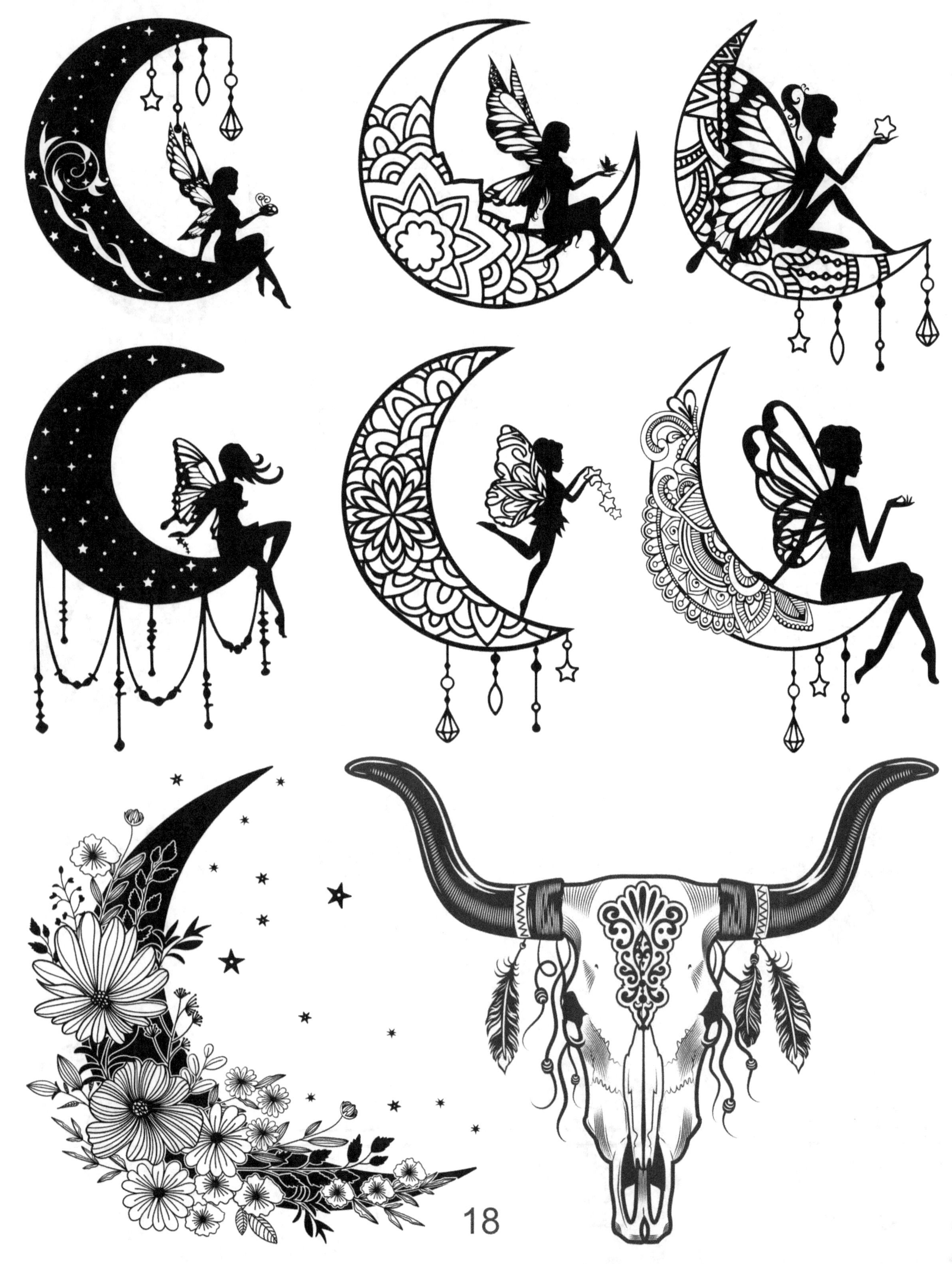

18

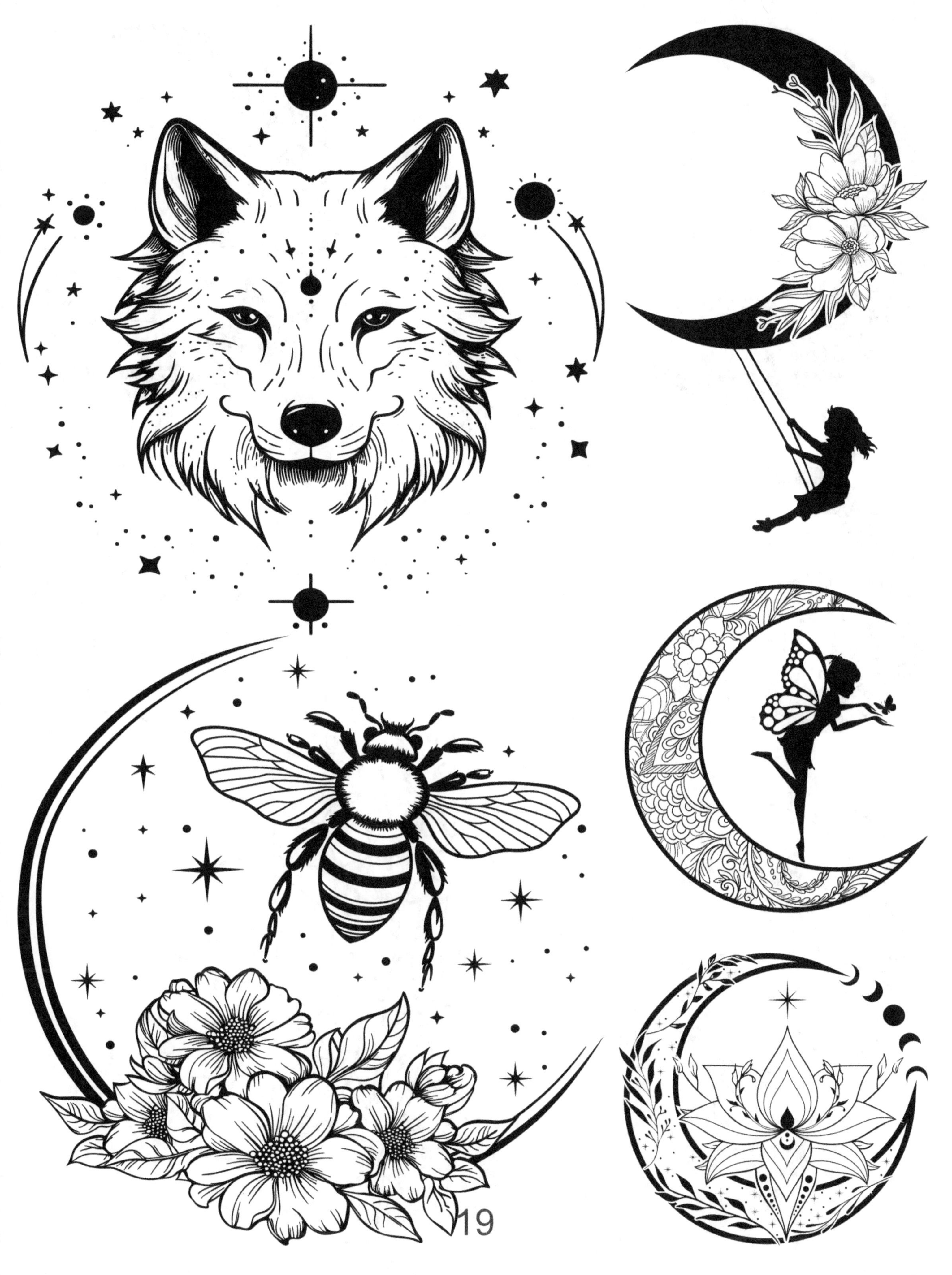

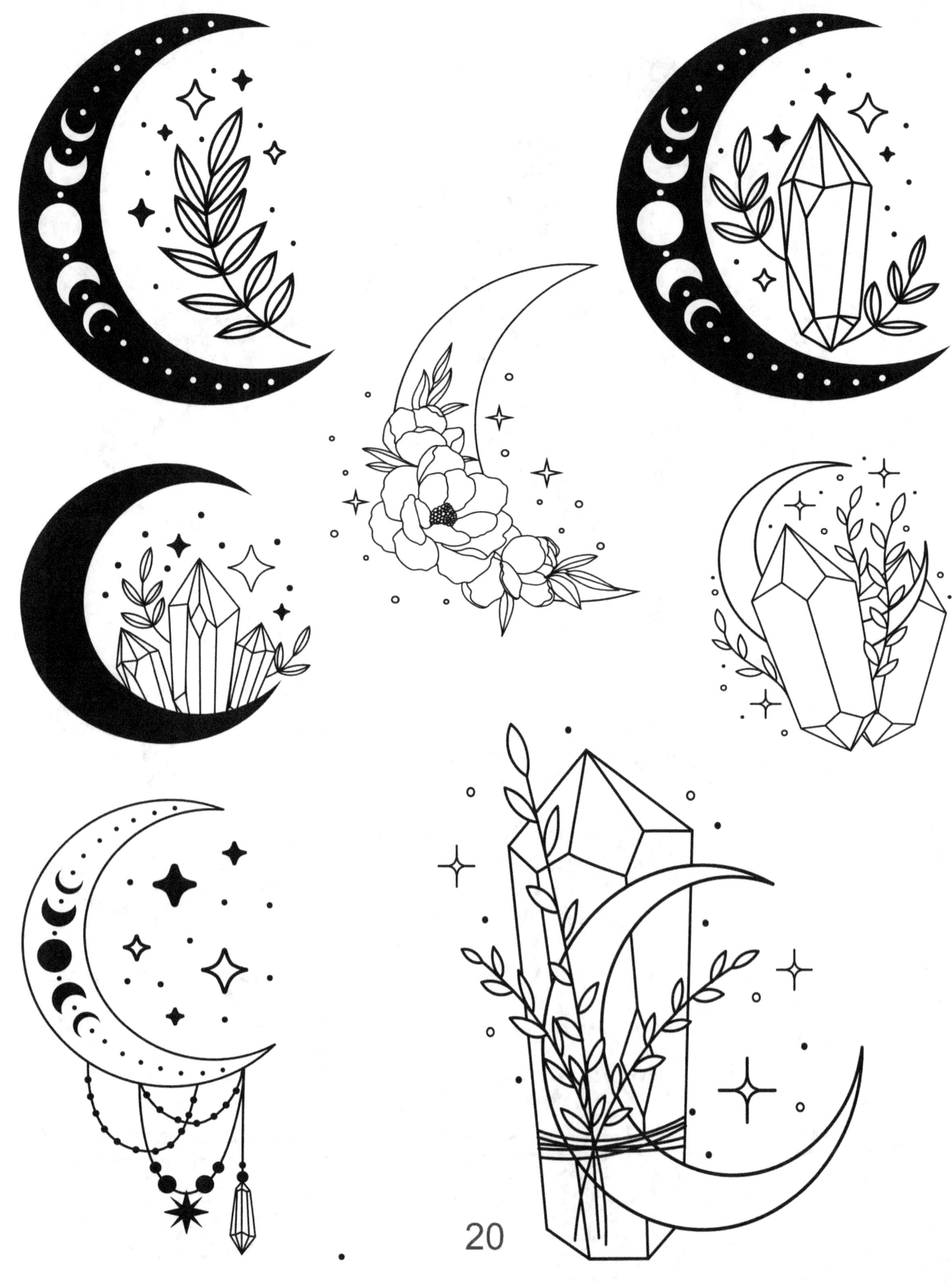

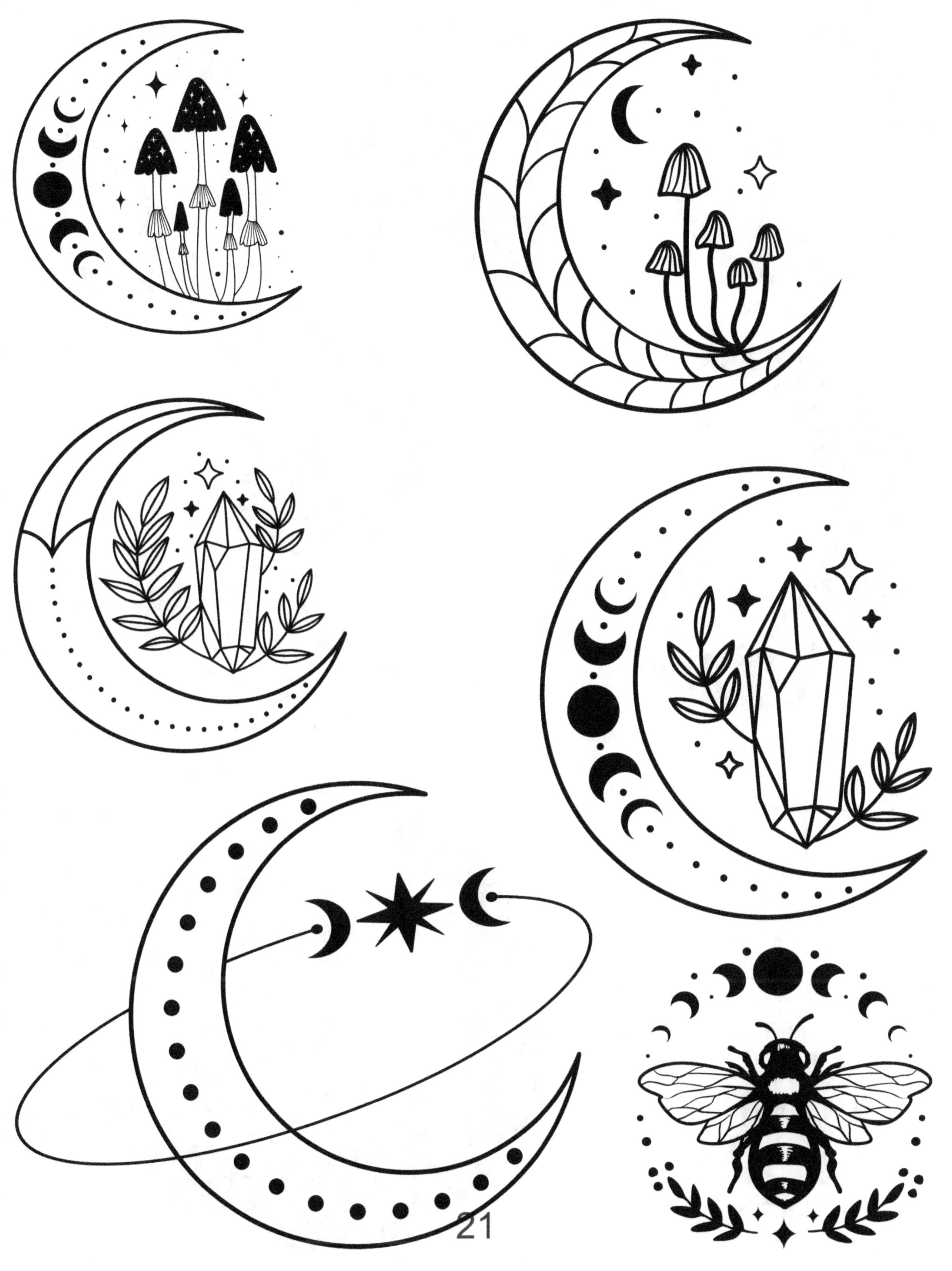

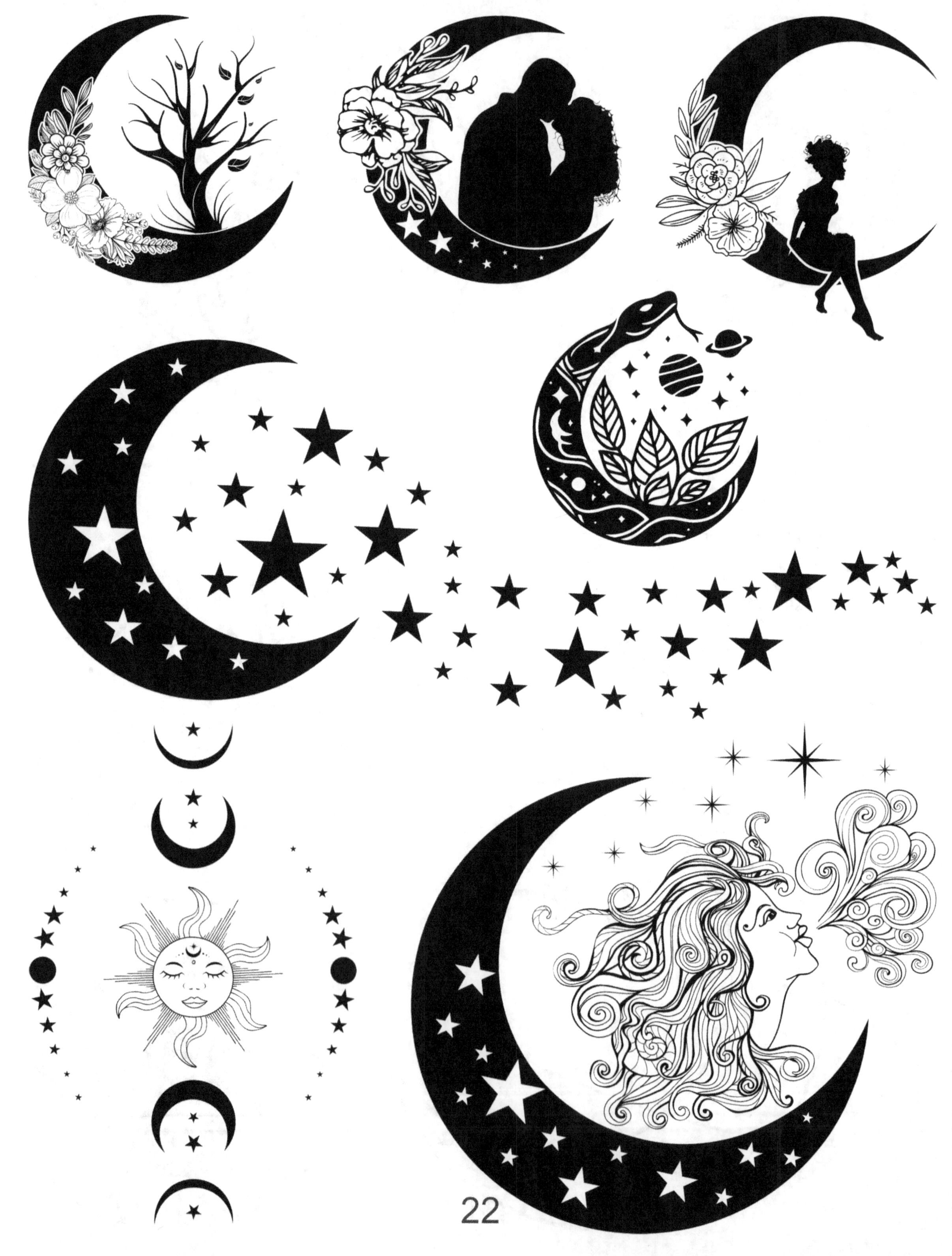

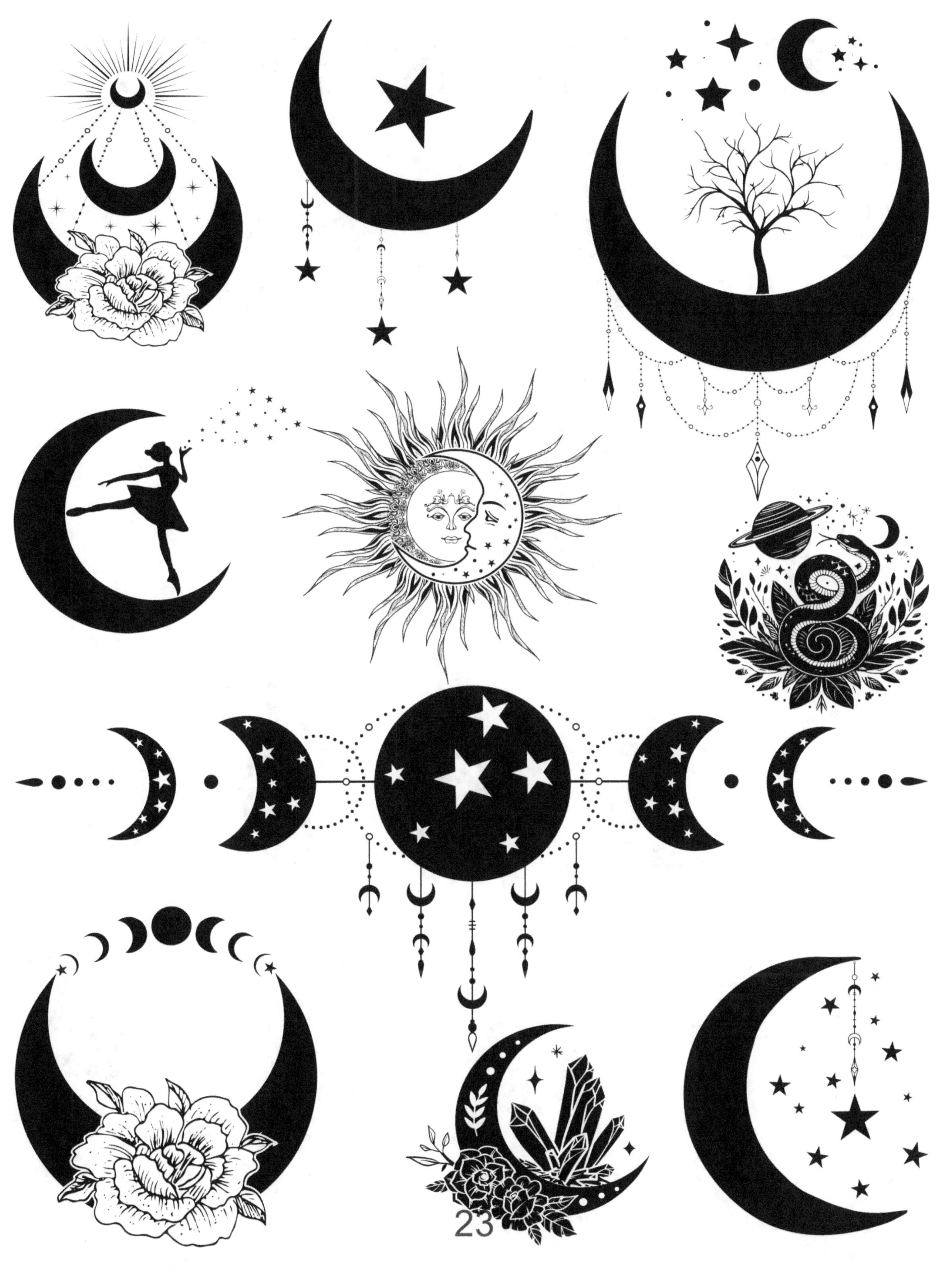

SNAKE TATTOOS

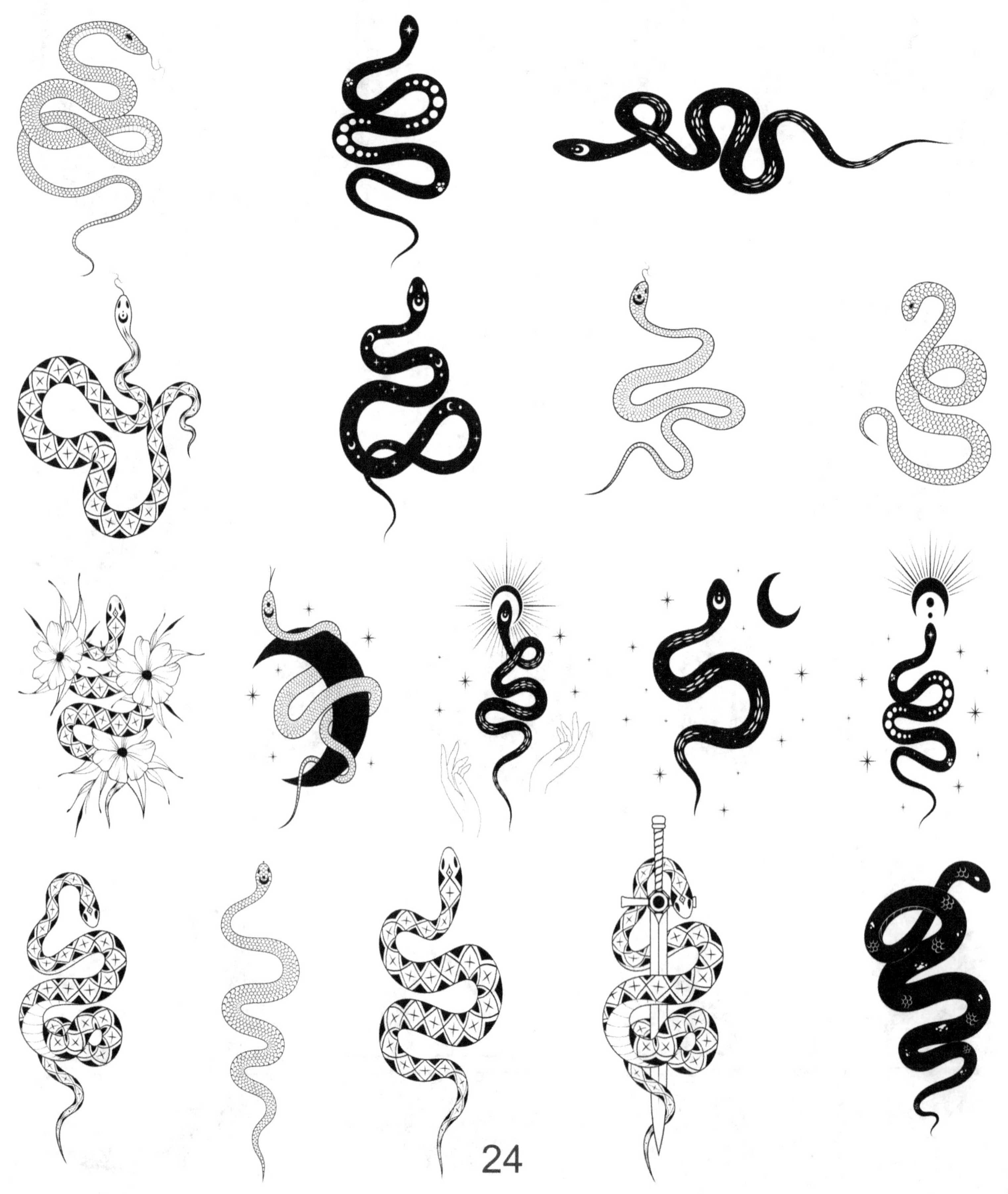

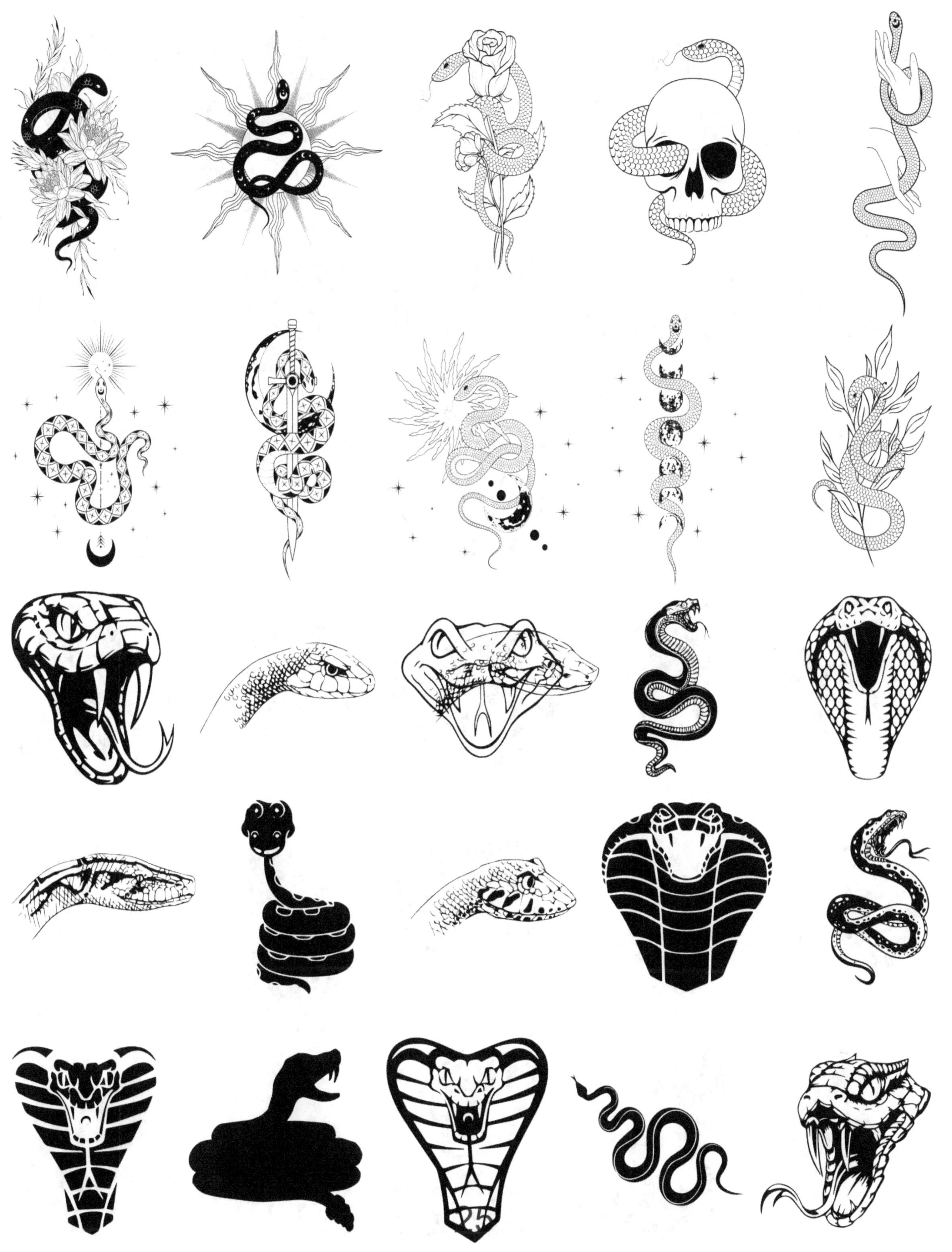

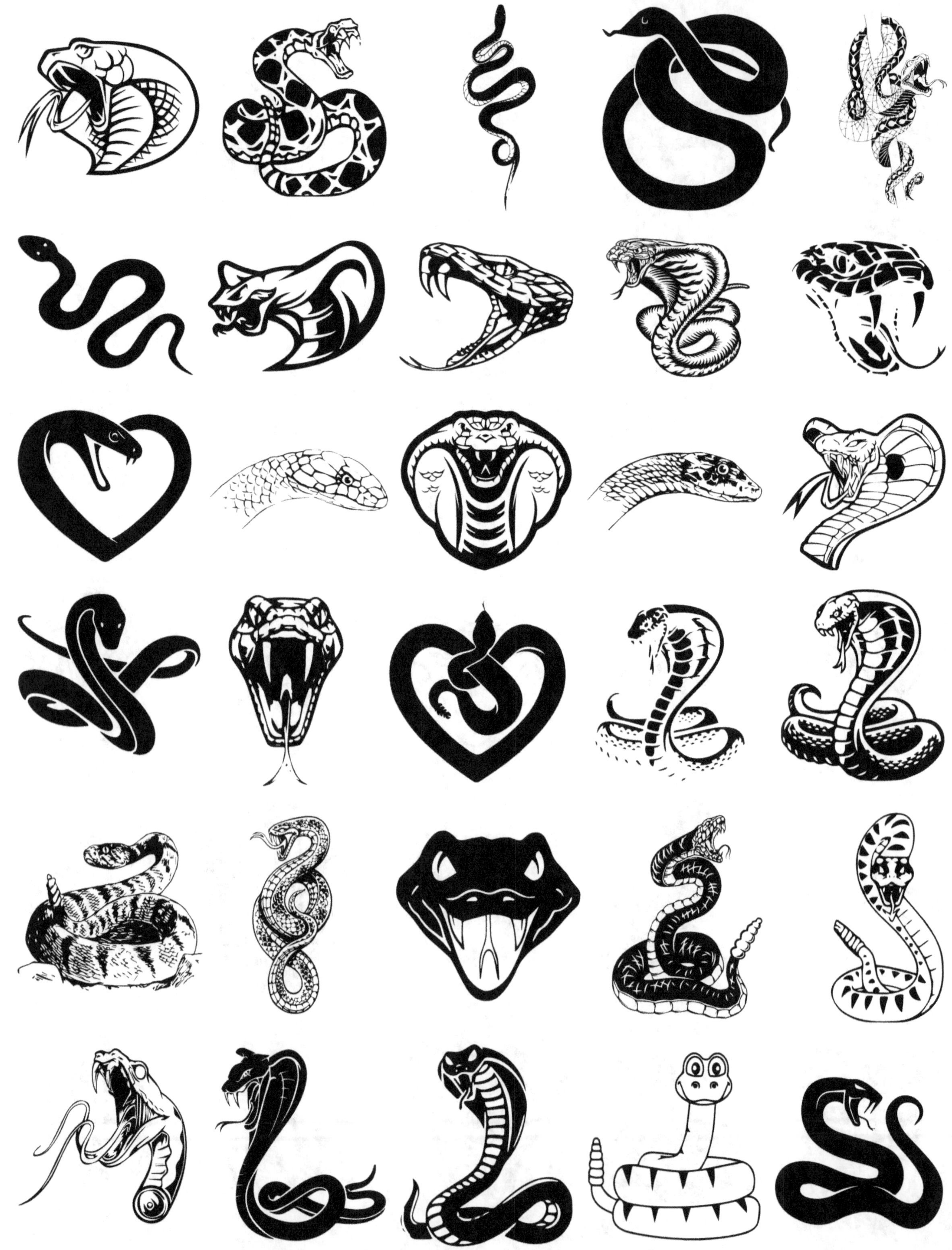

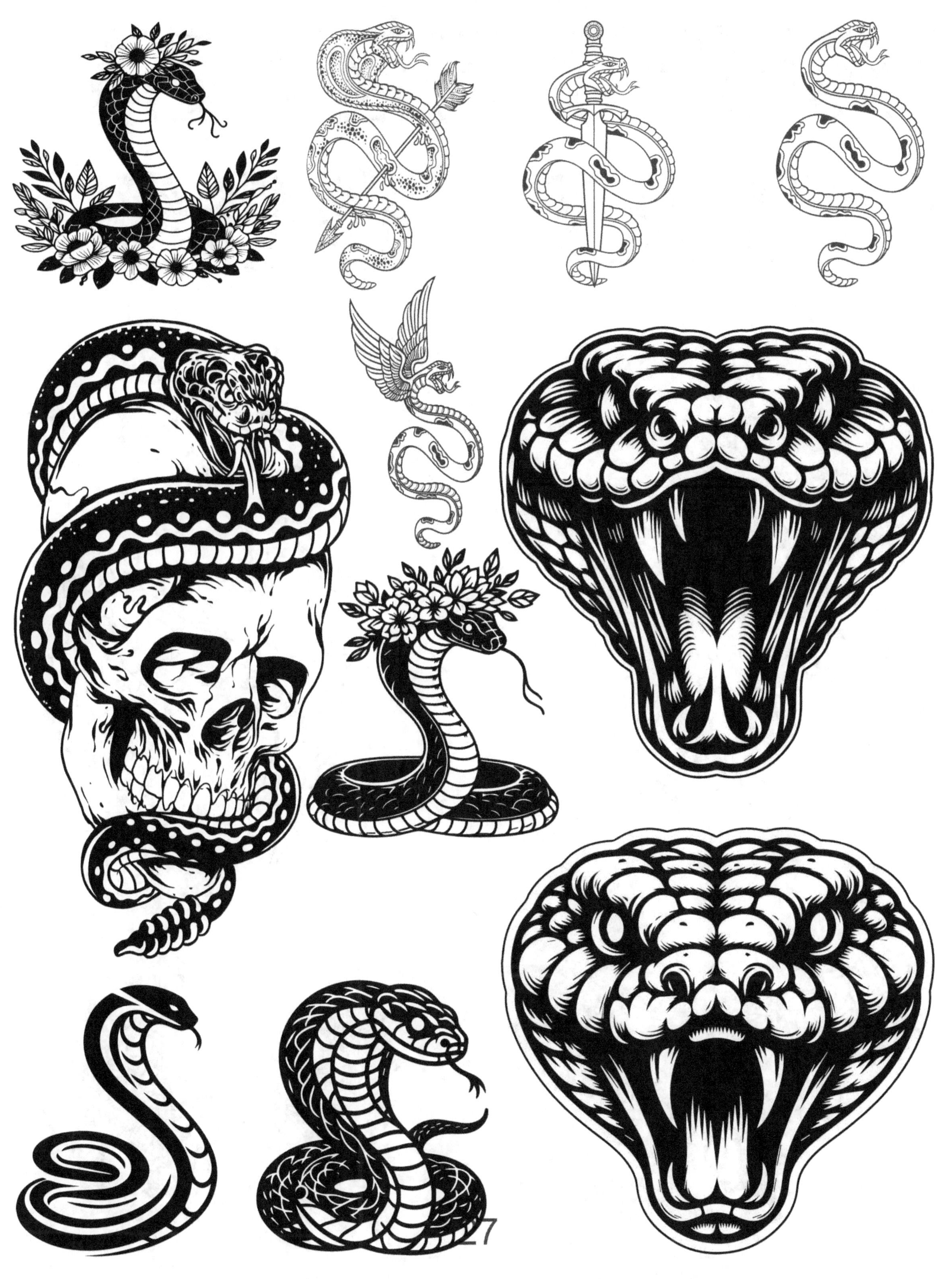

BUTTERFLY TATTOOS

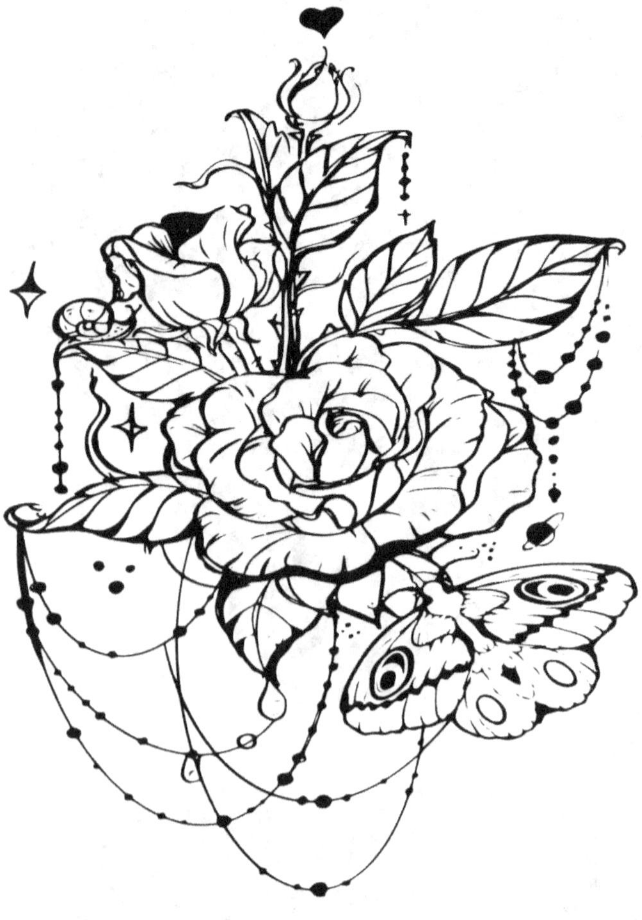

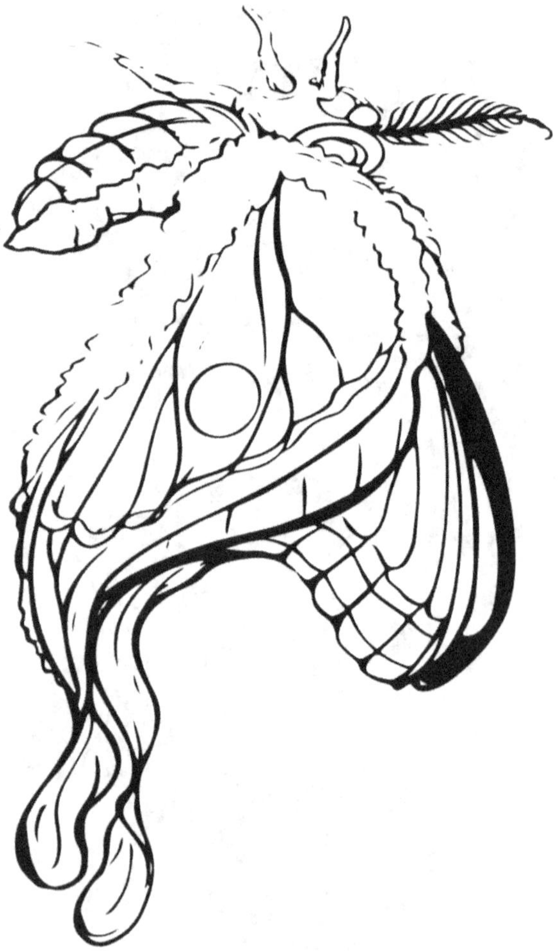

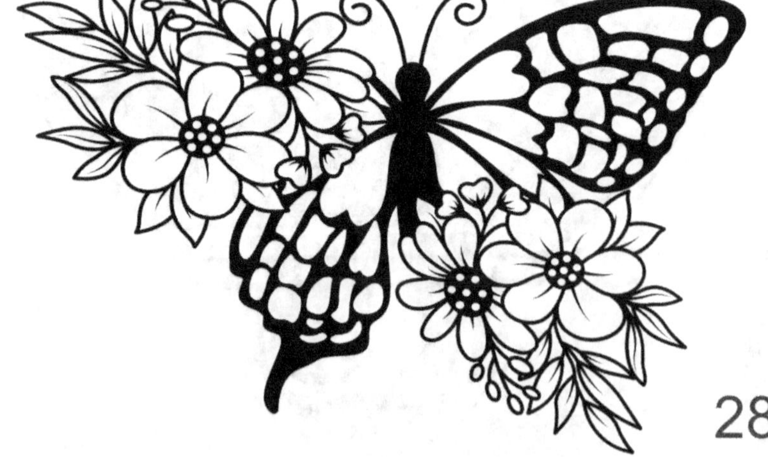

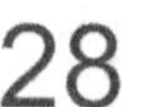

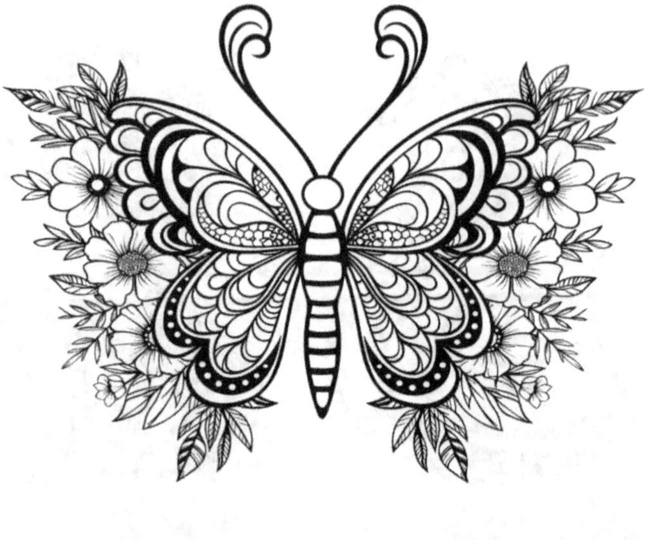

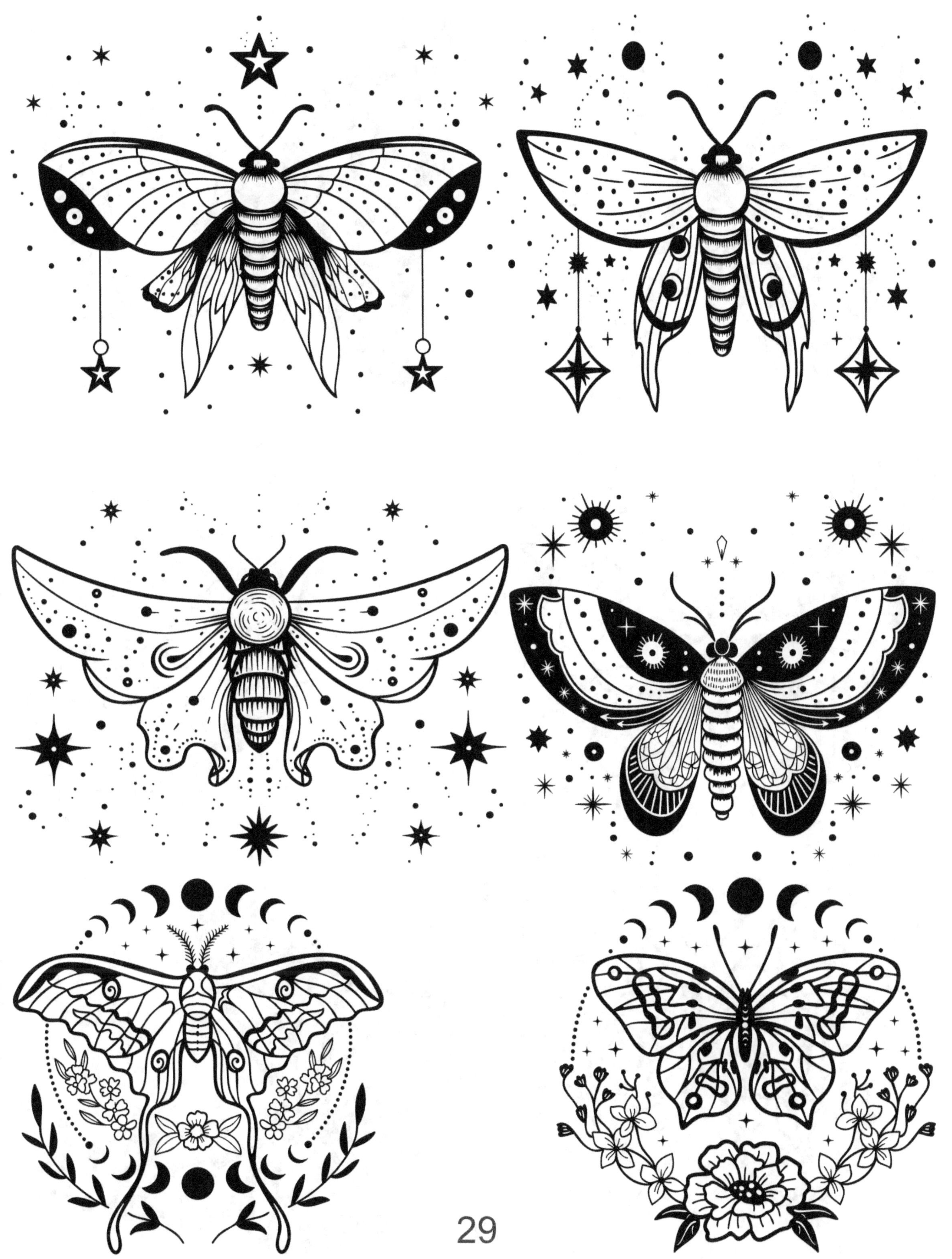

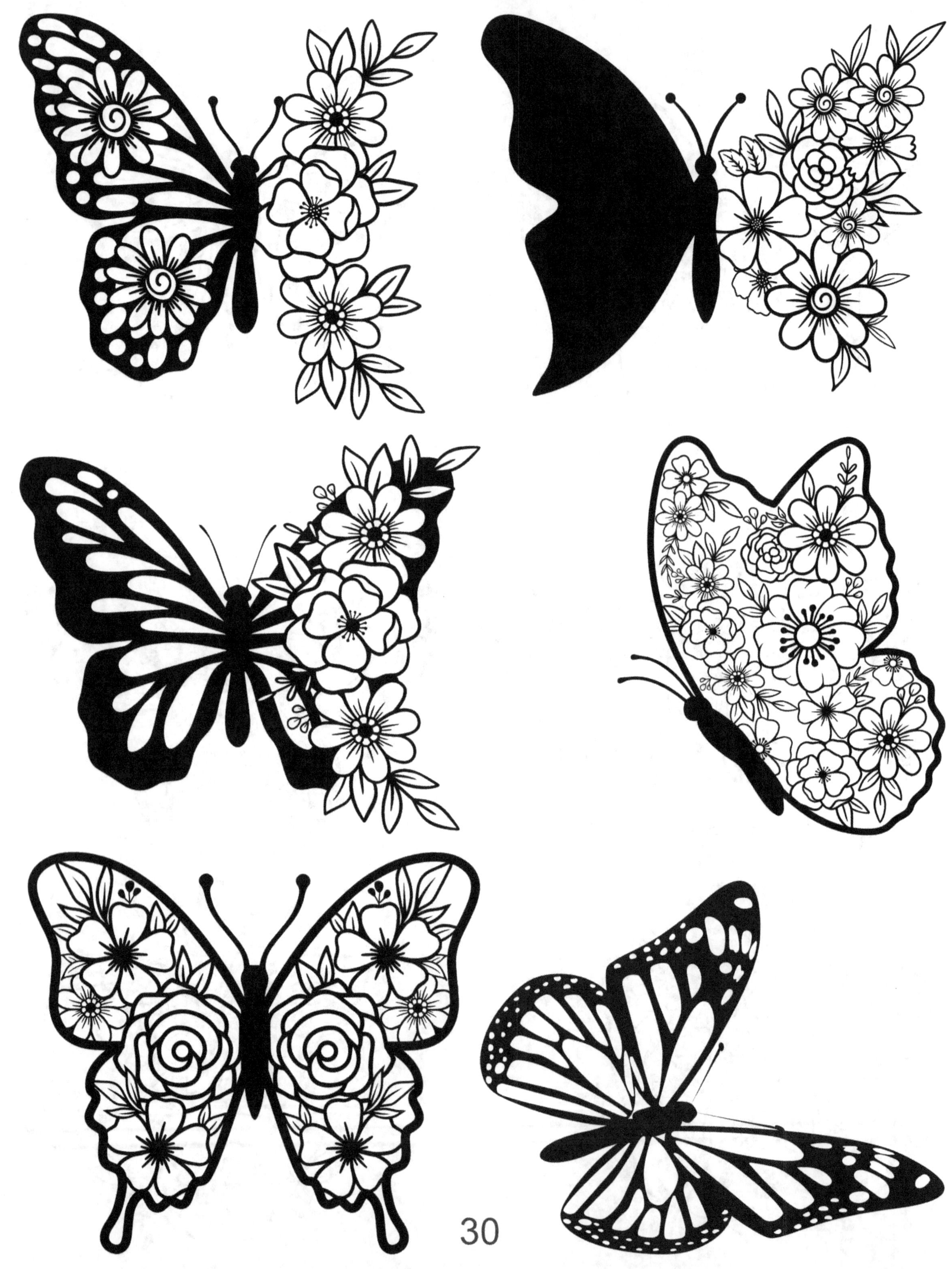

30

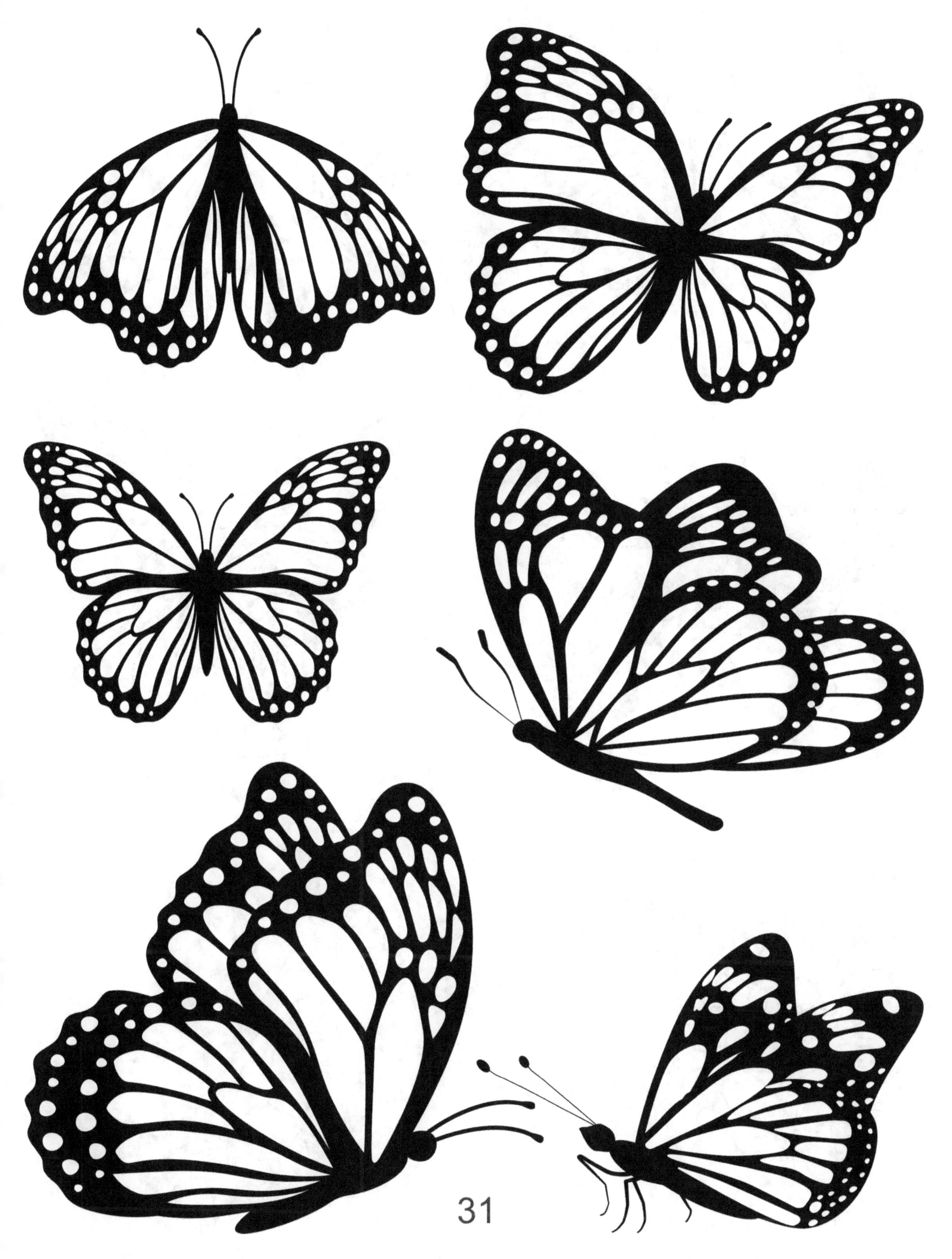

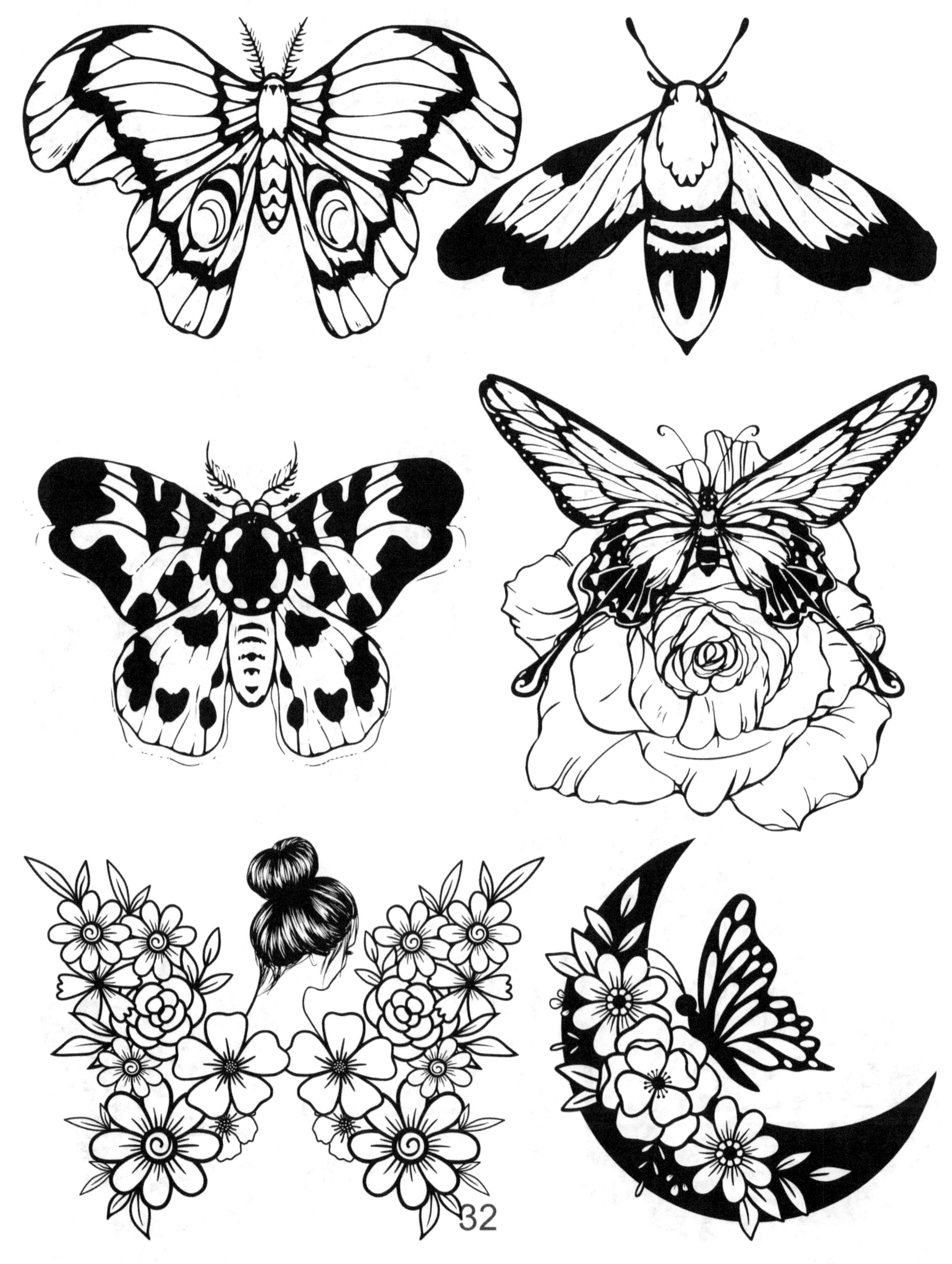

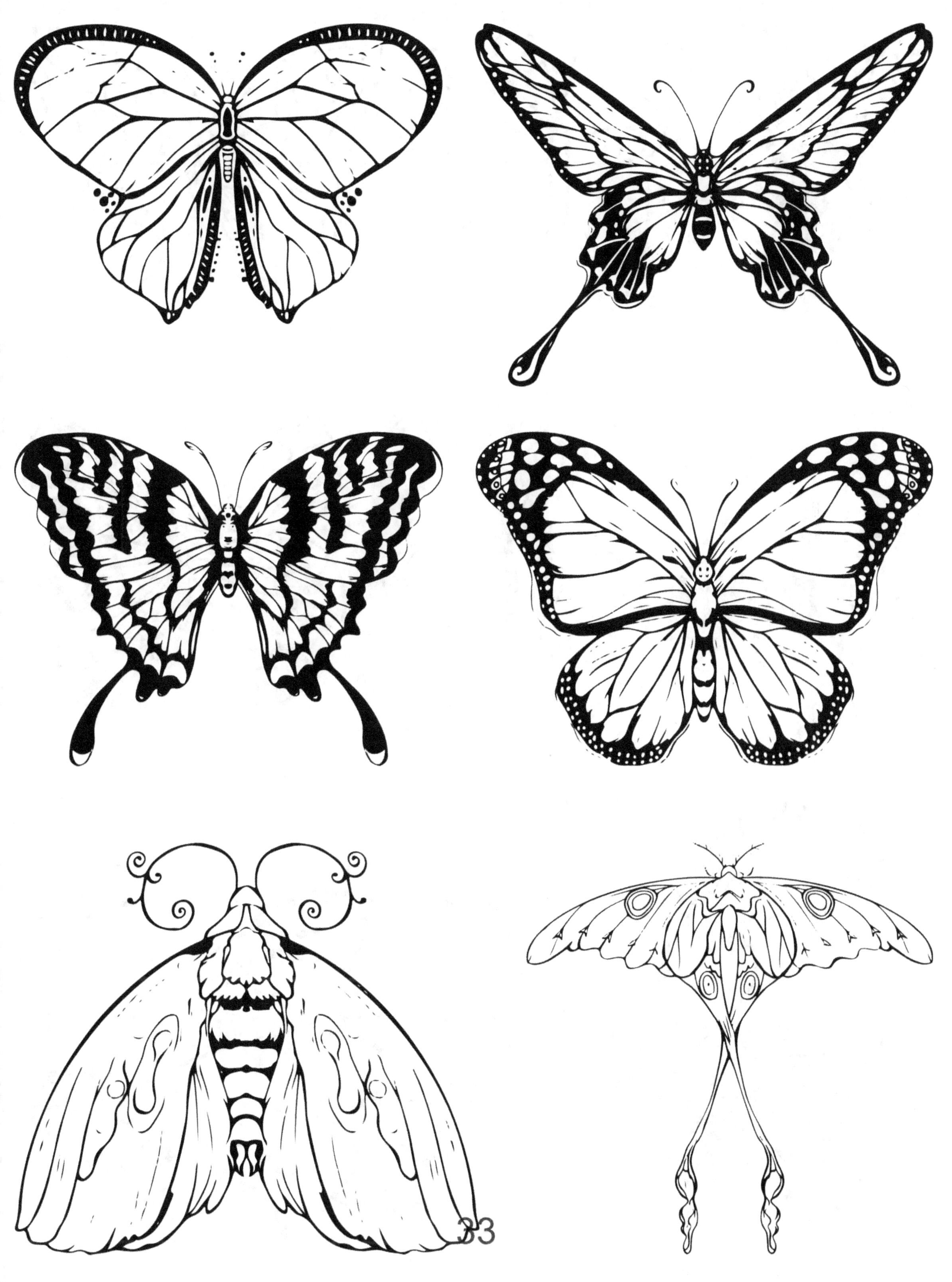

33

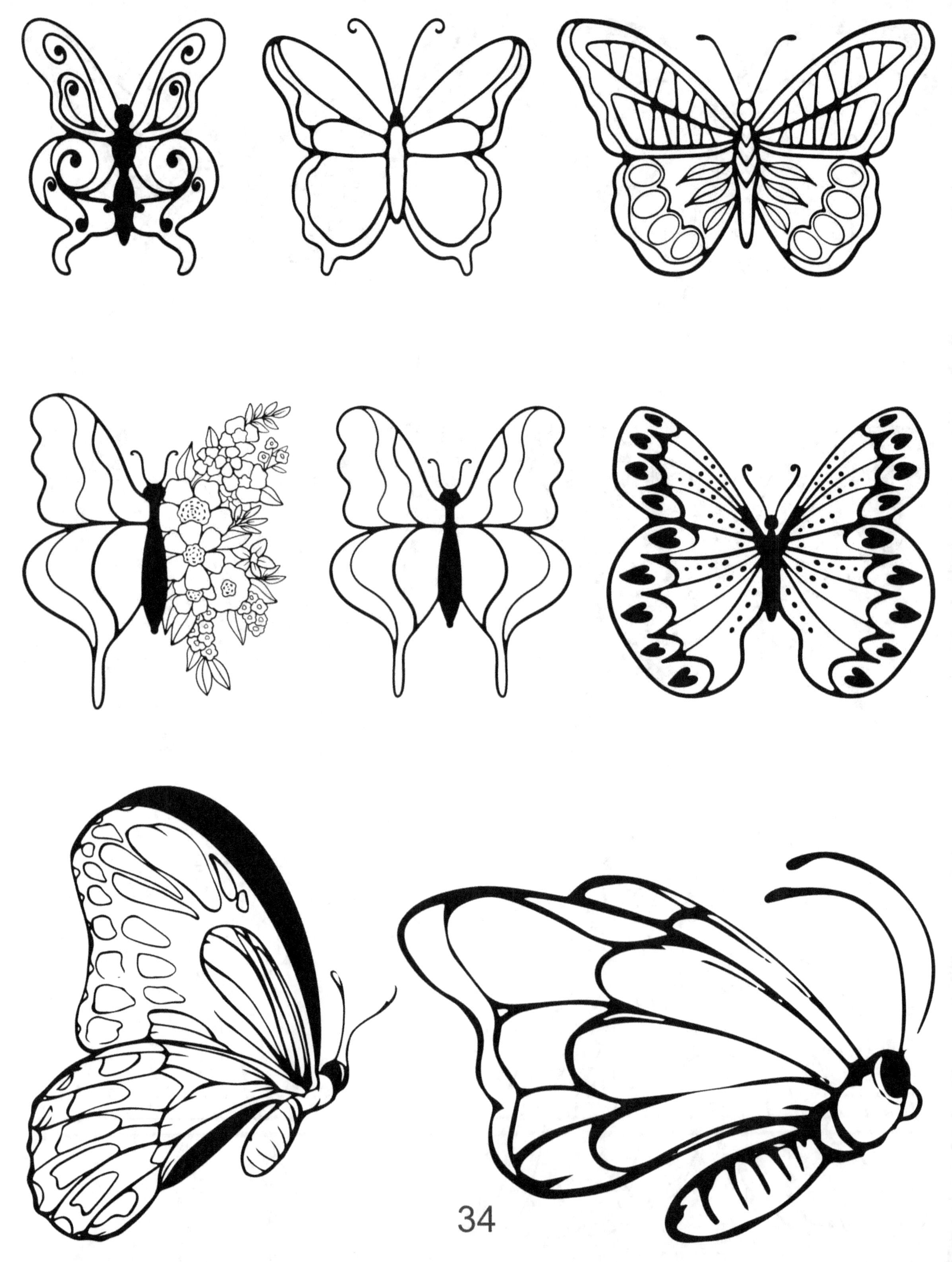

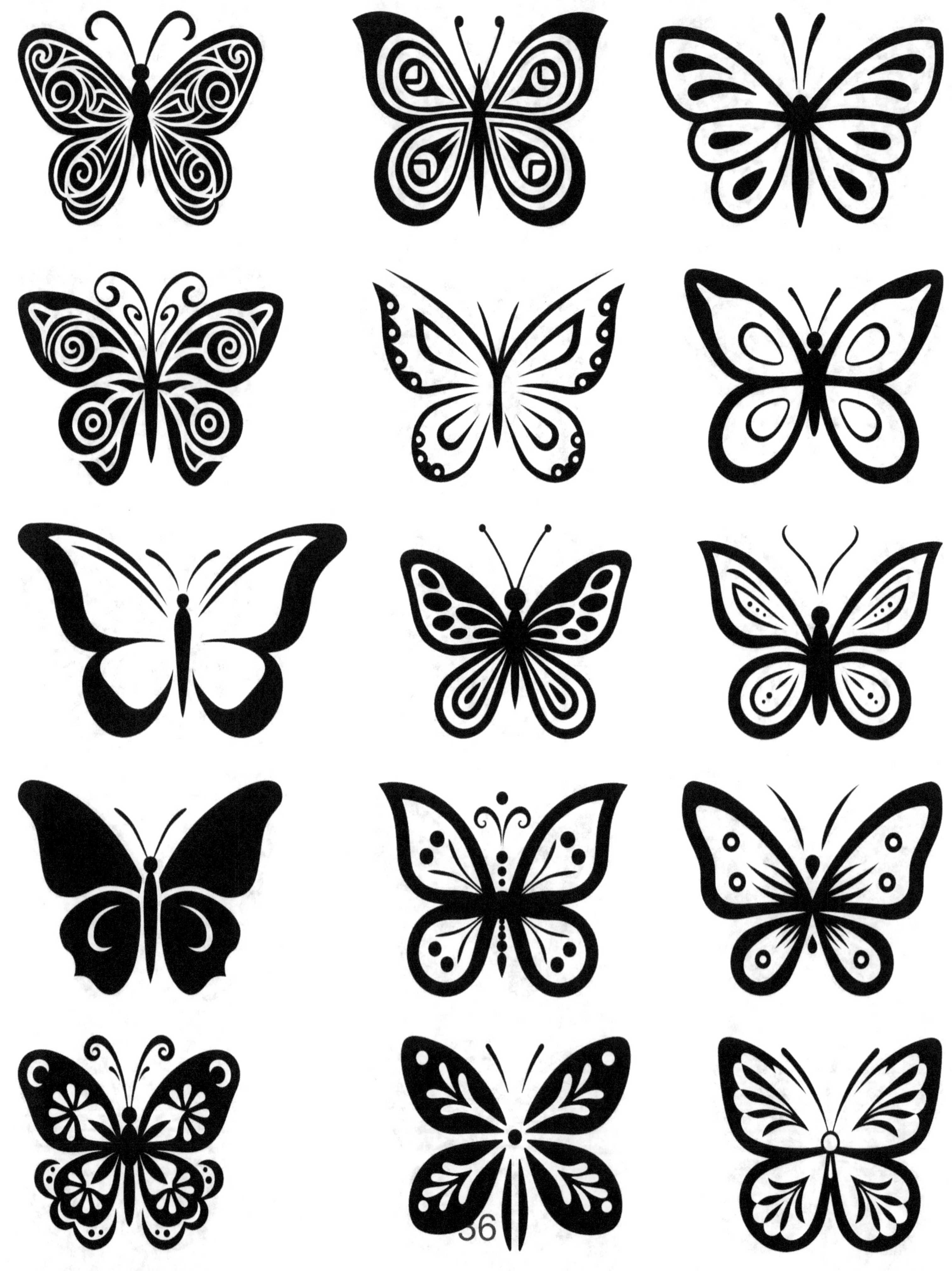

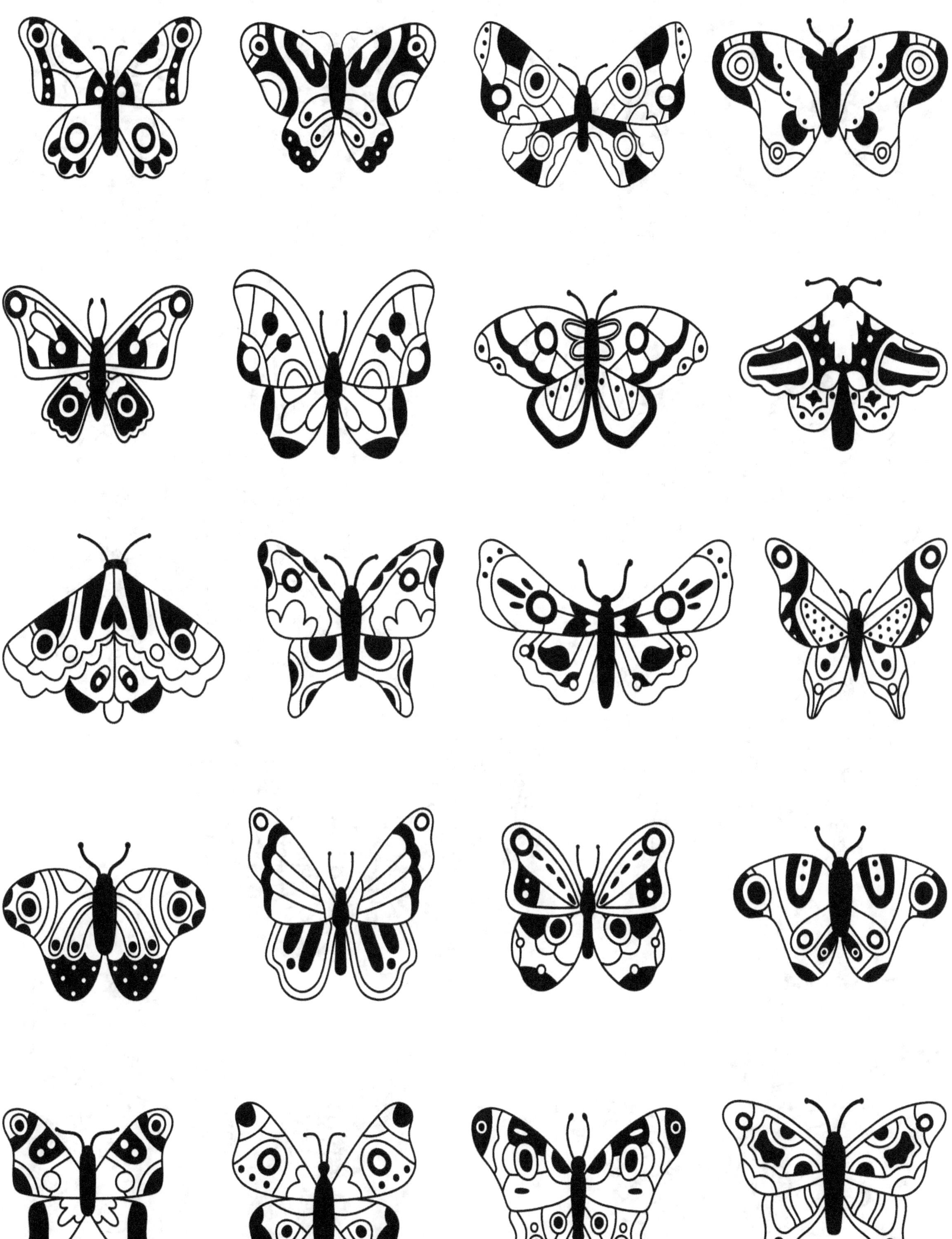

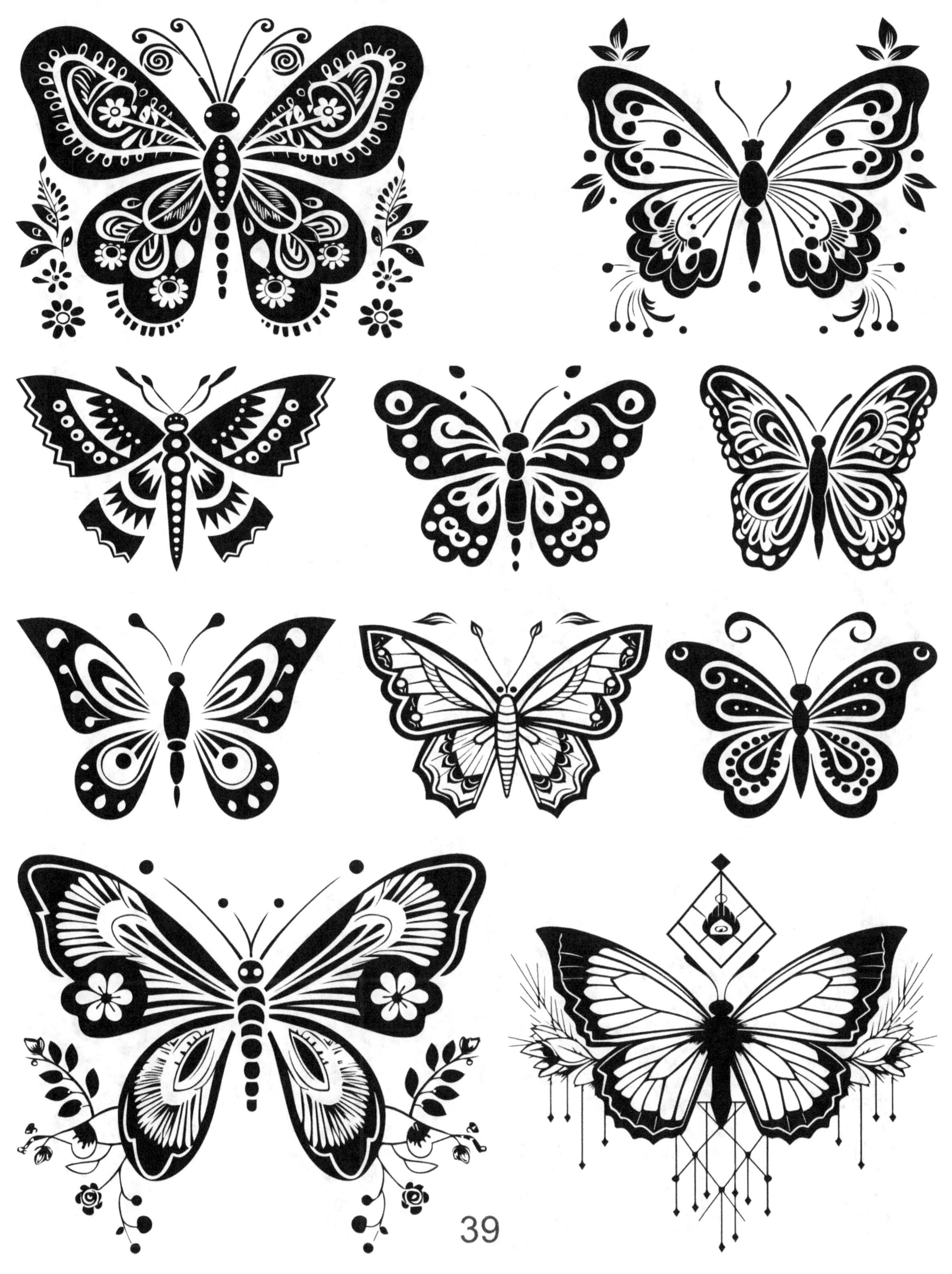

39

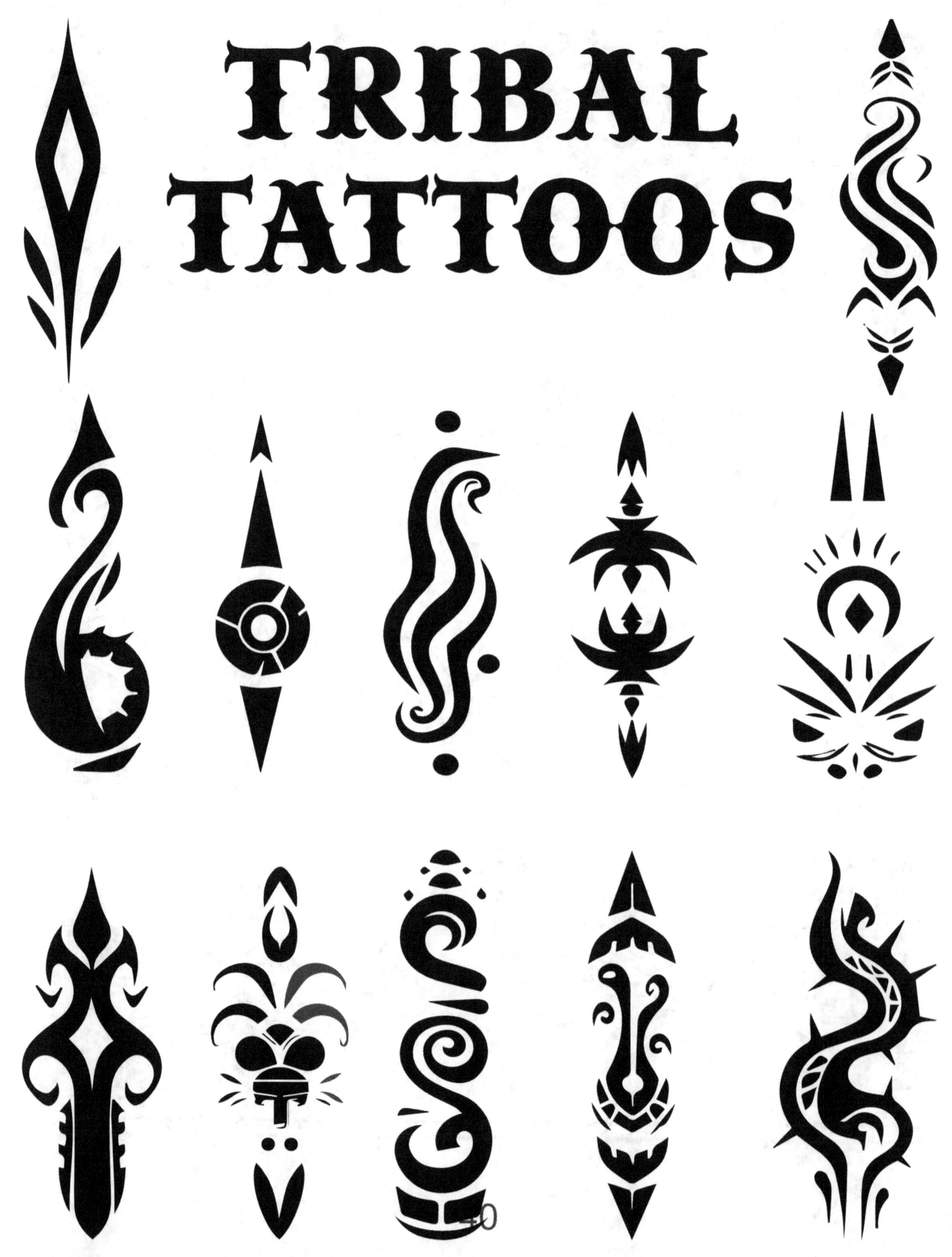

TRIBAL
TATTOOS

41

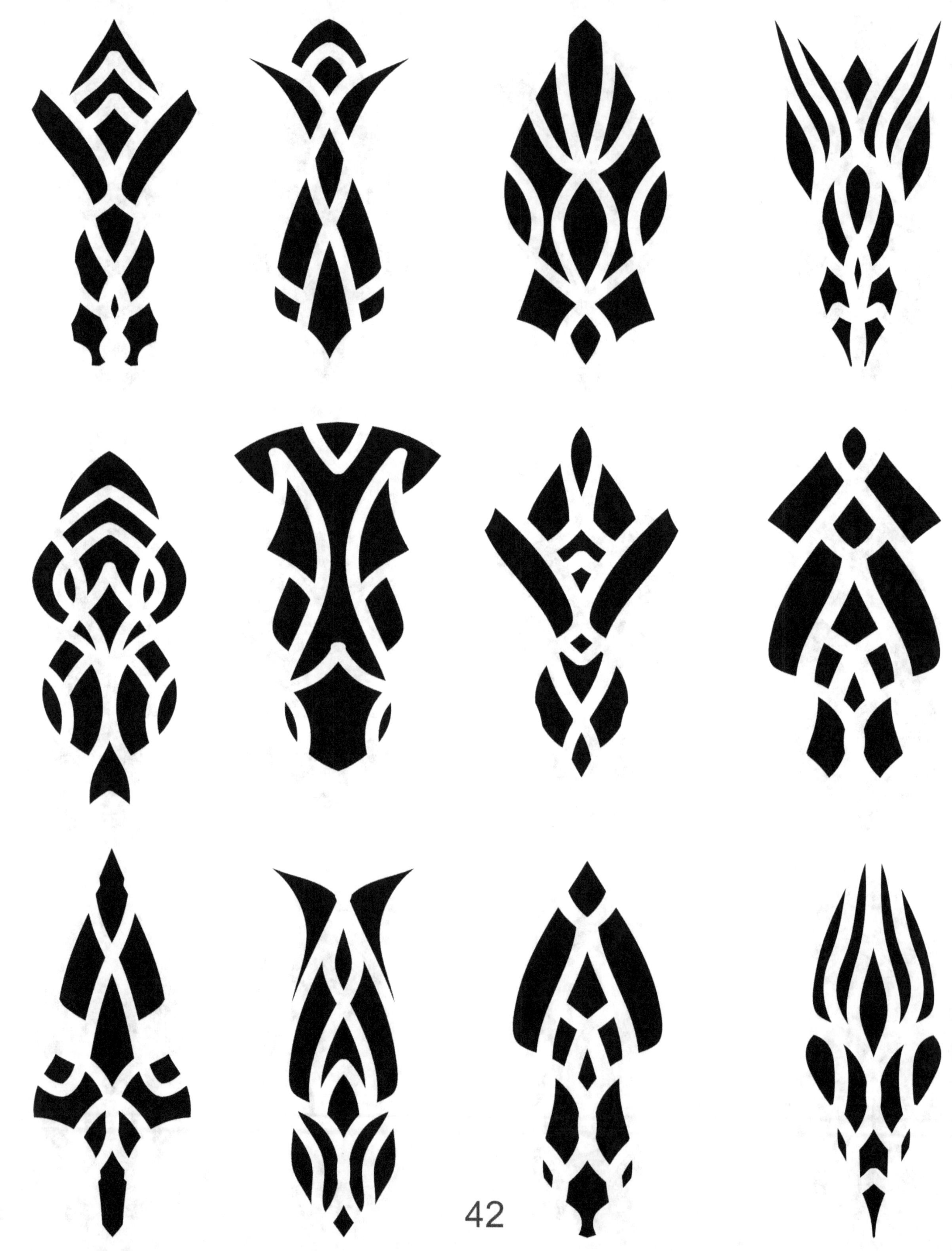

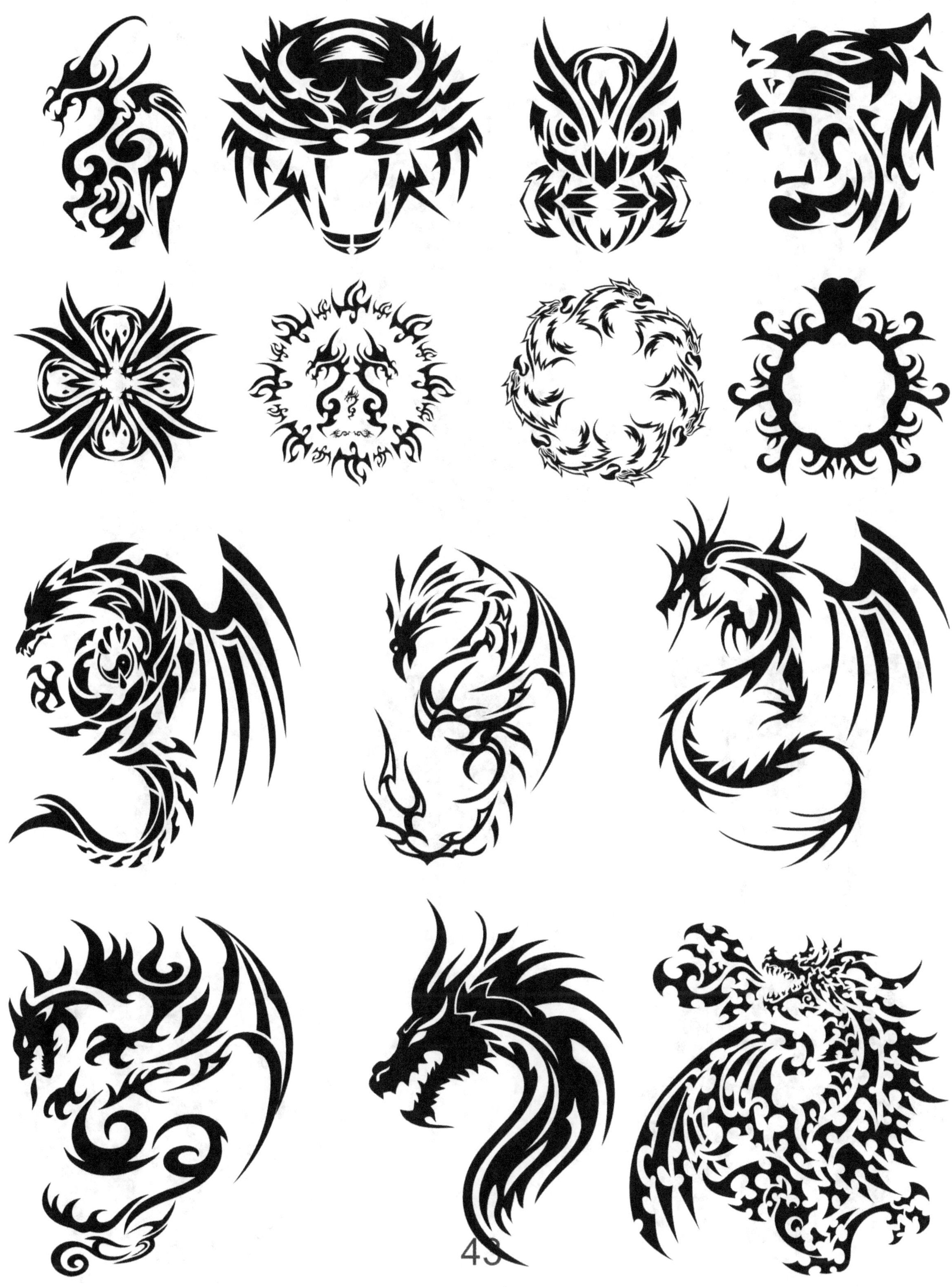

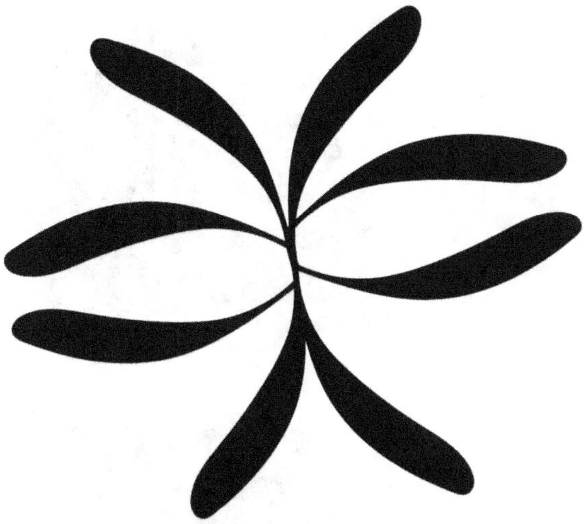

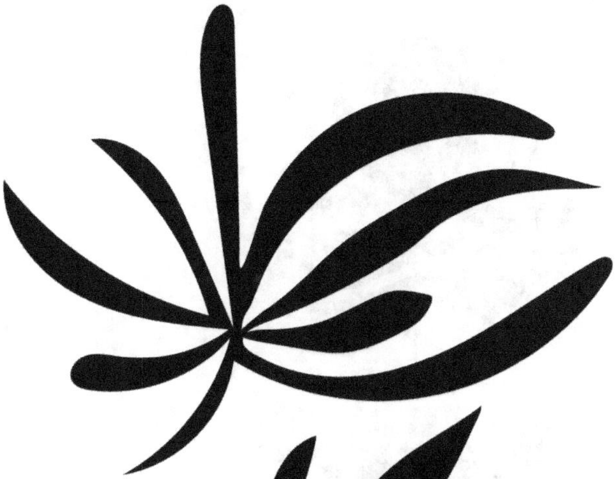

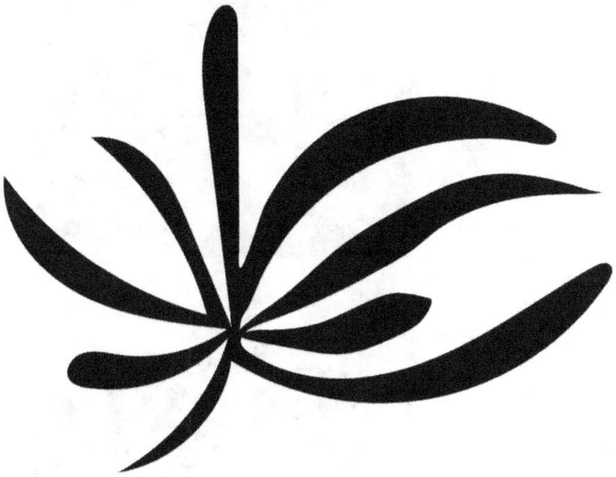

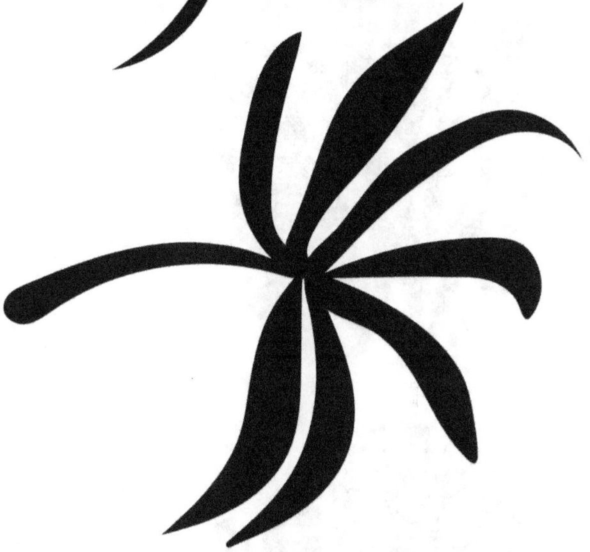

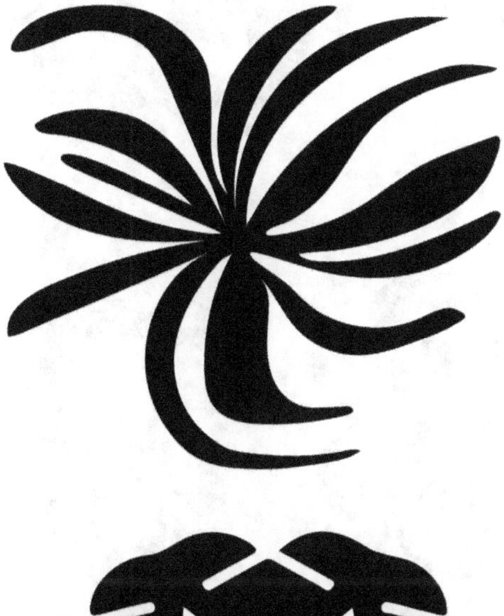

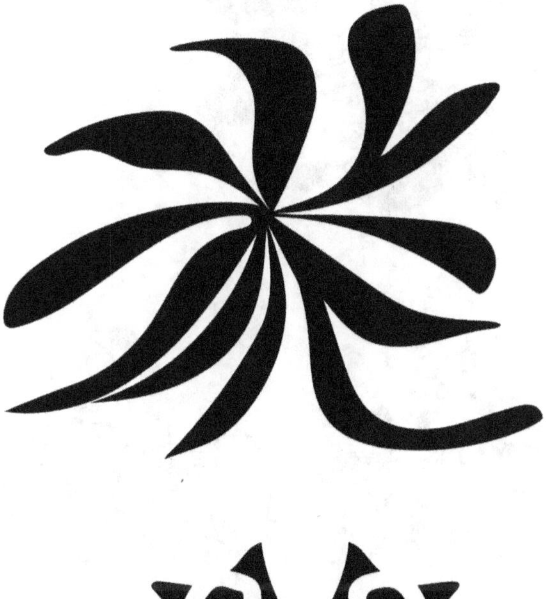

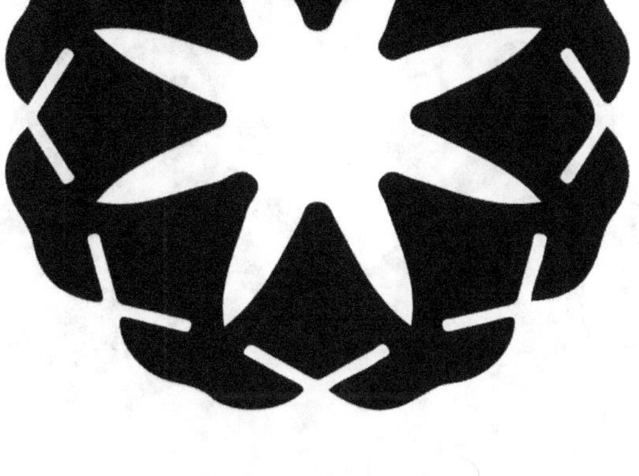

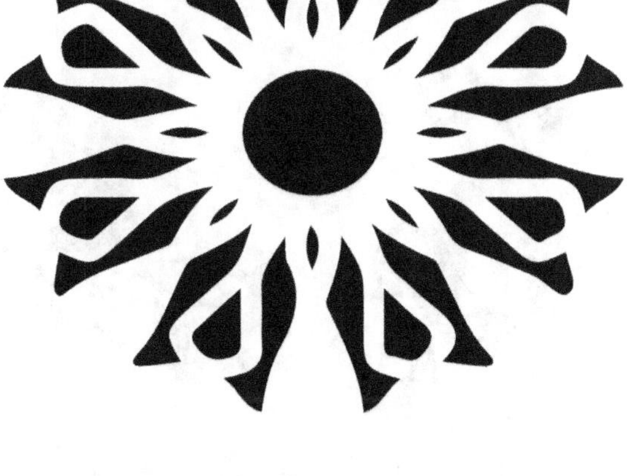

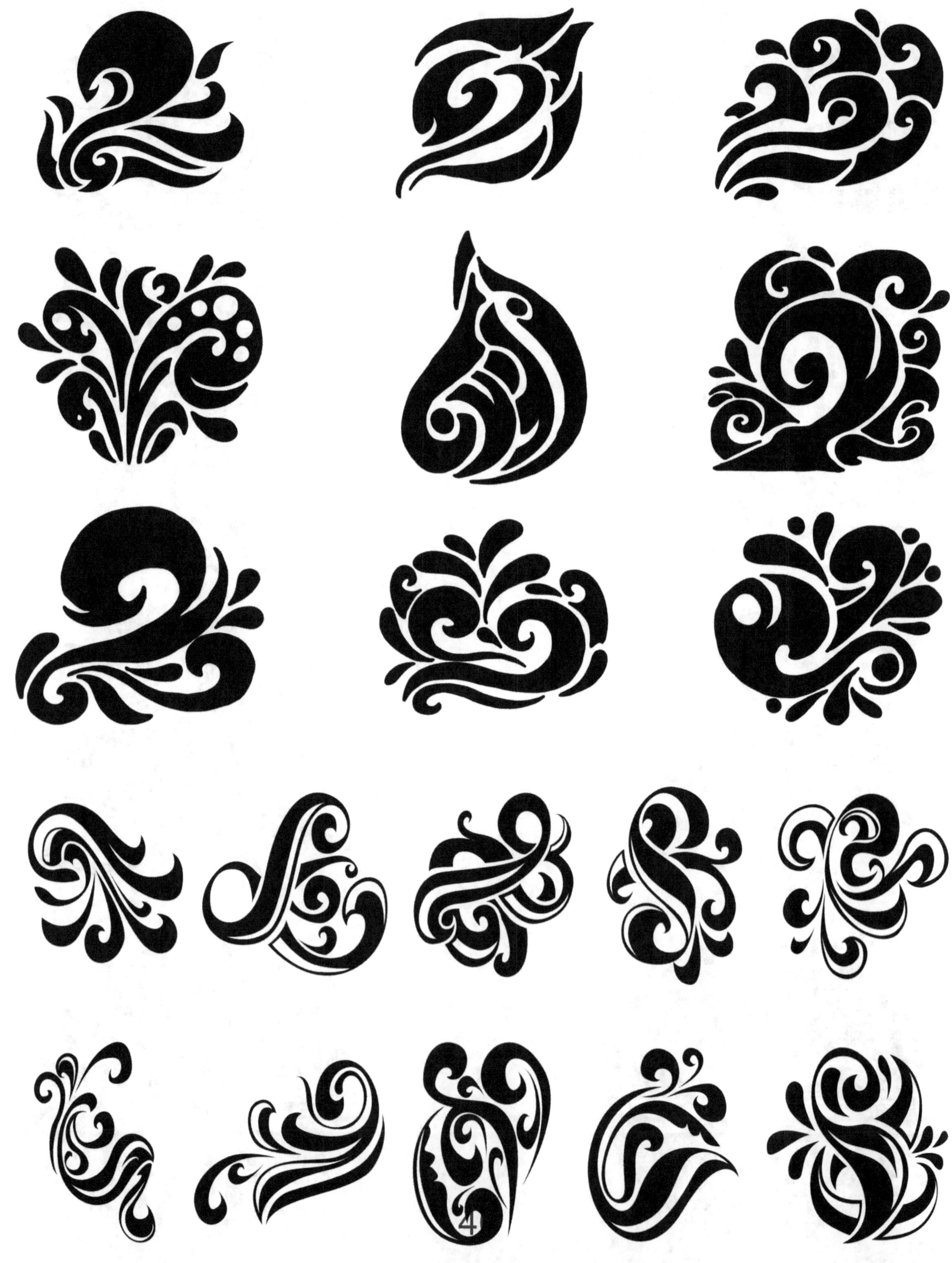

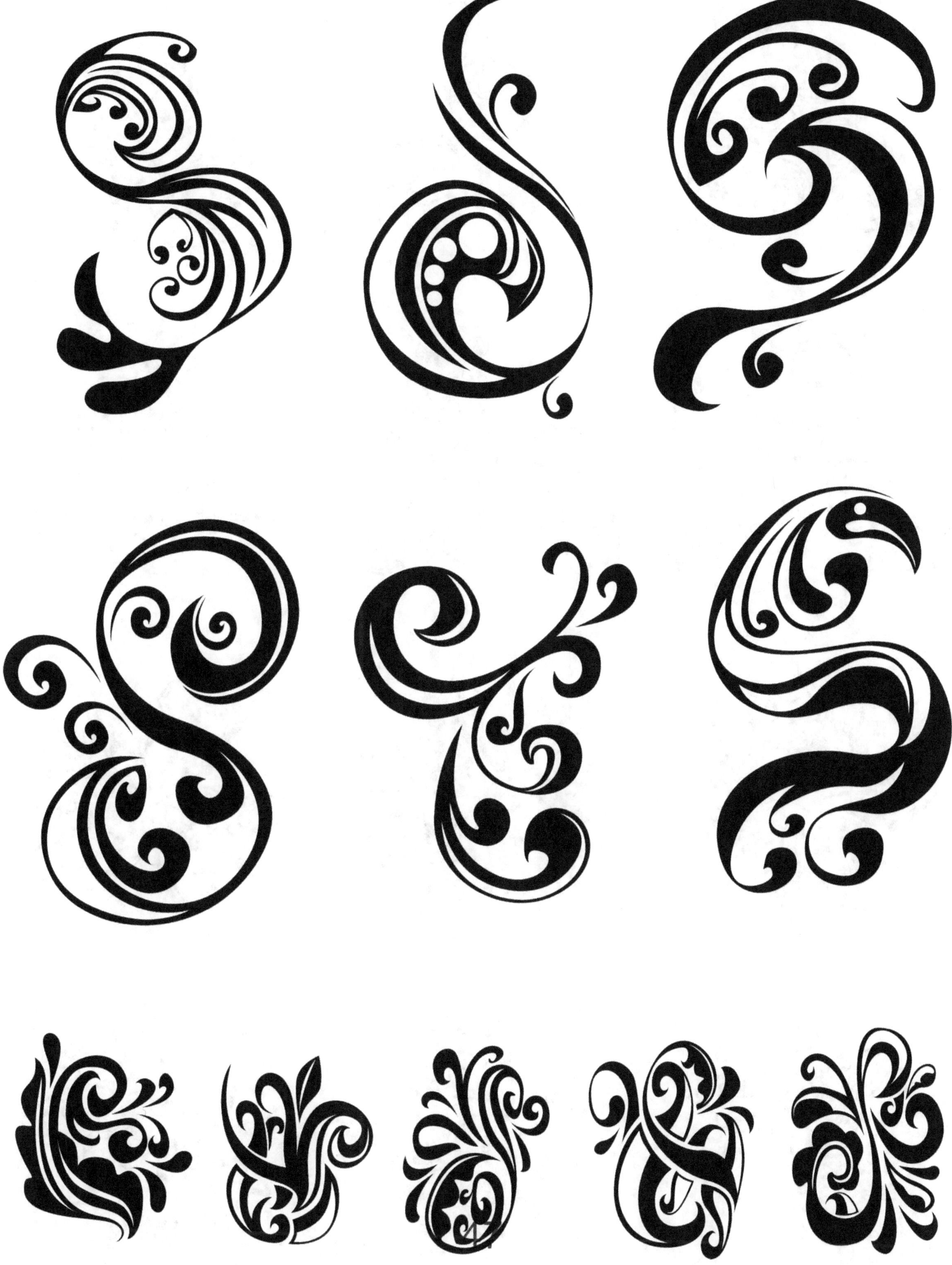

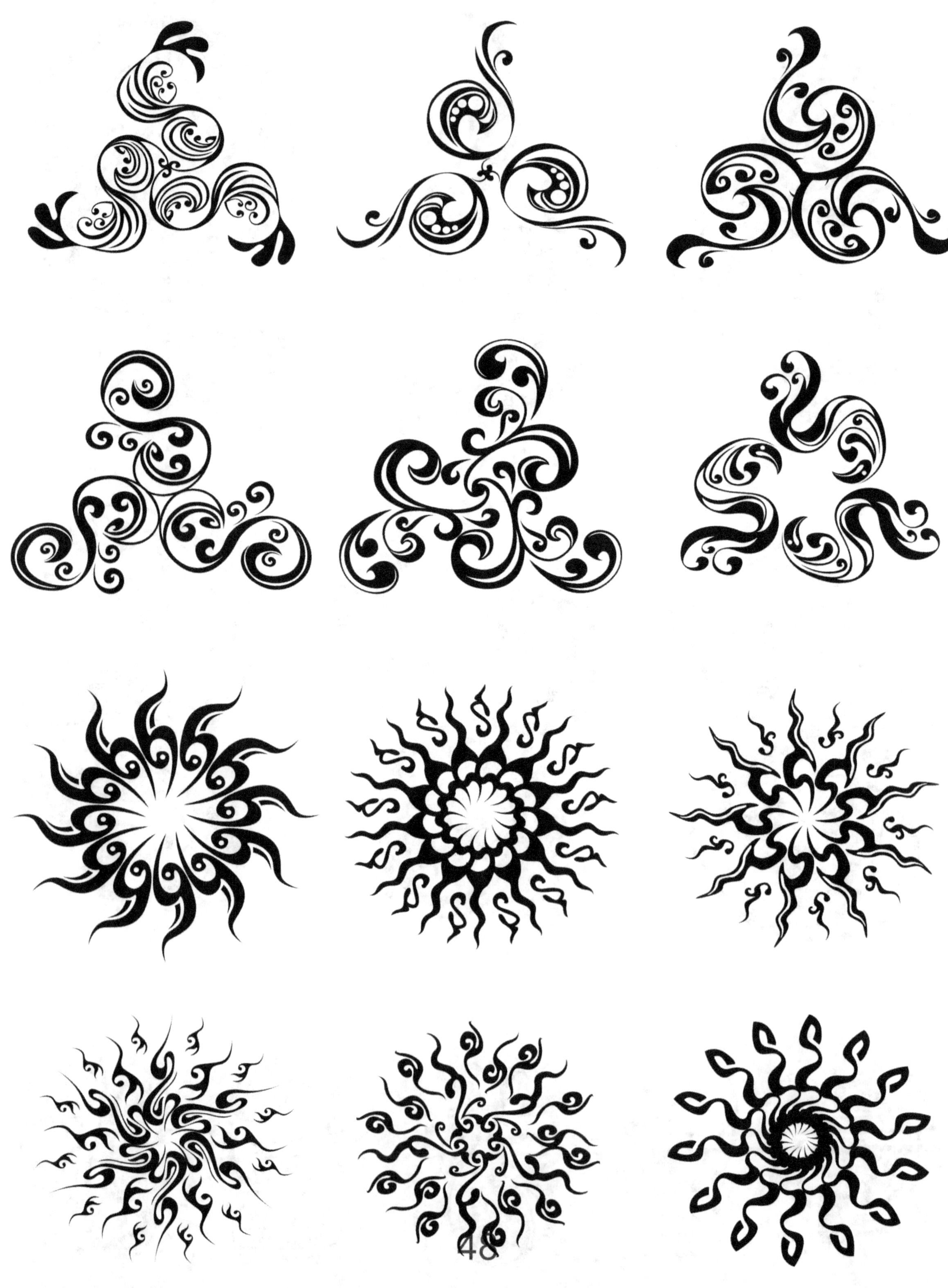

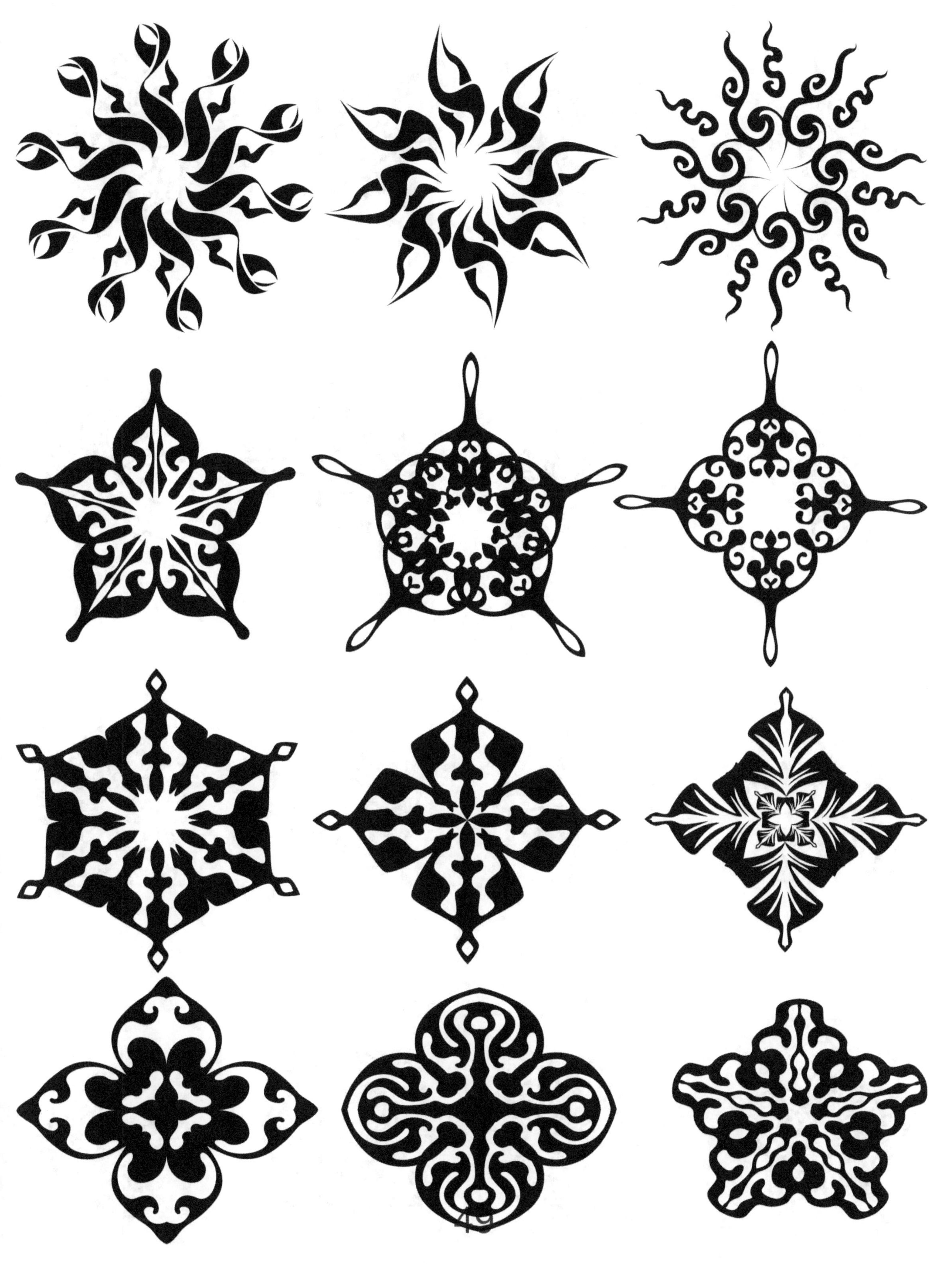

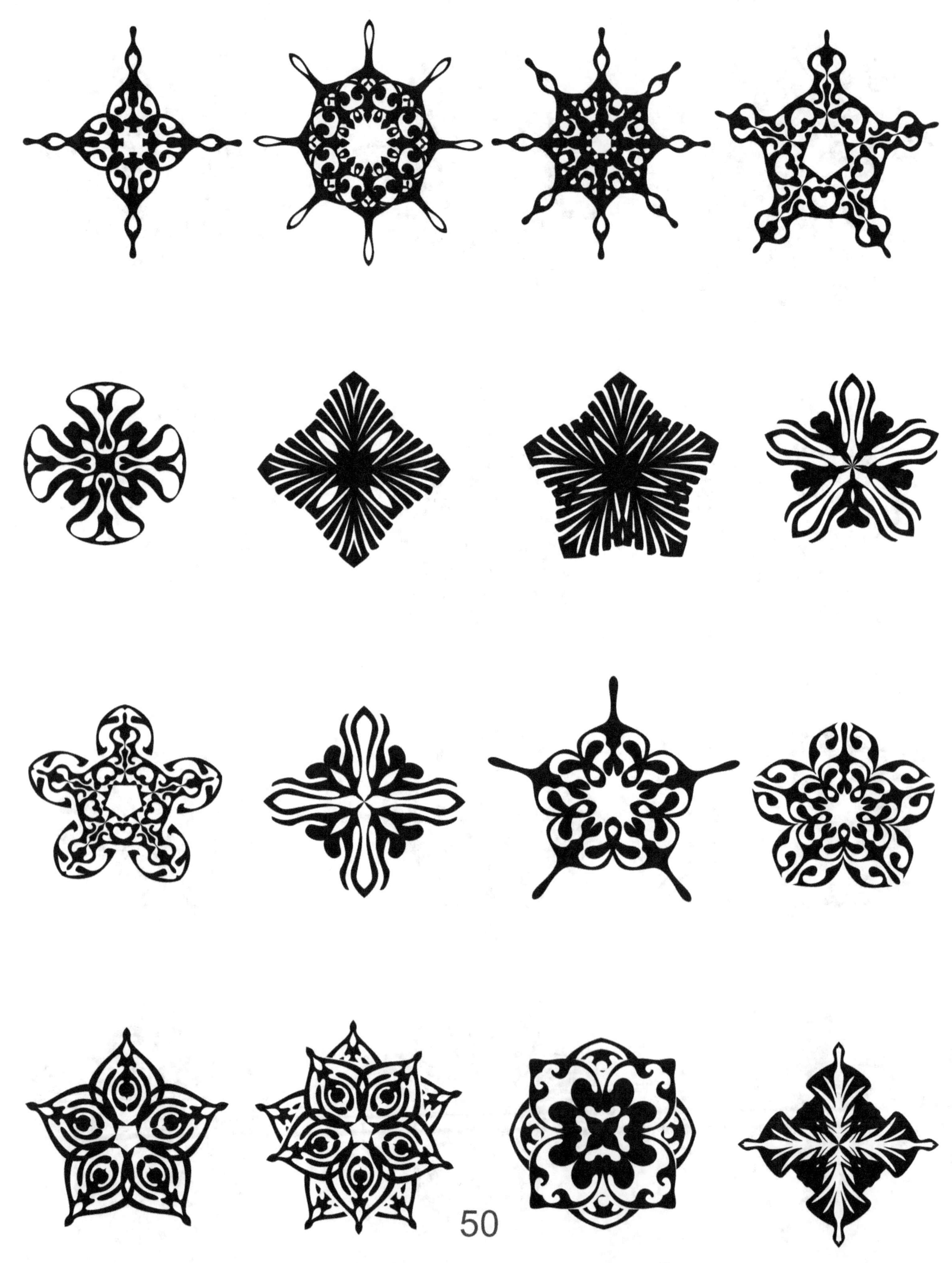

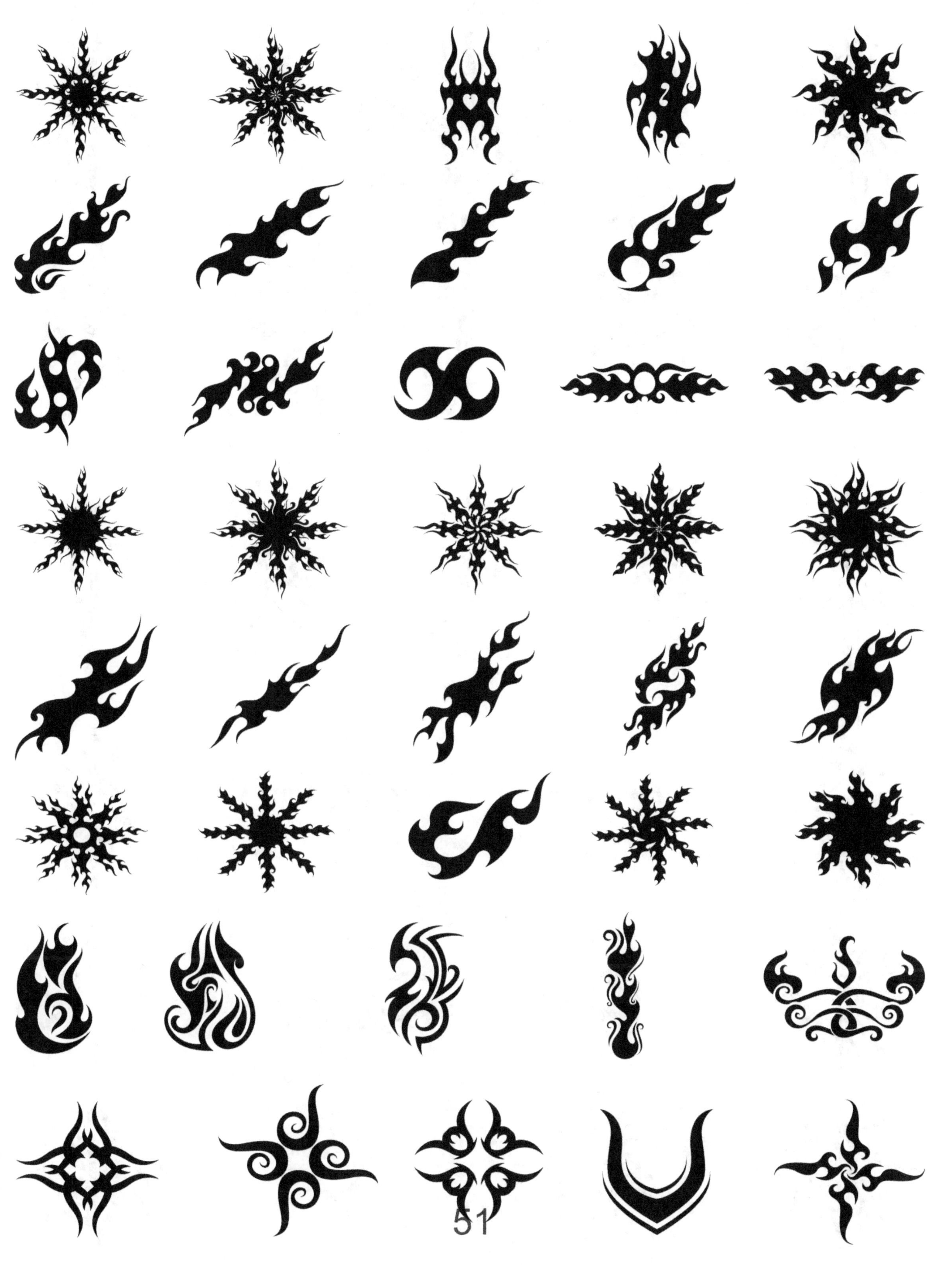

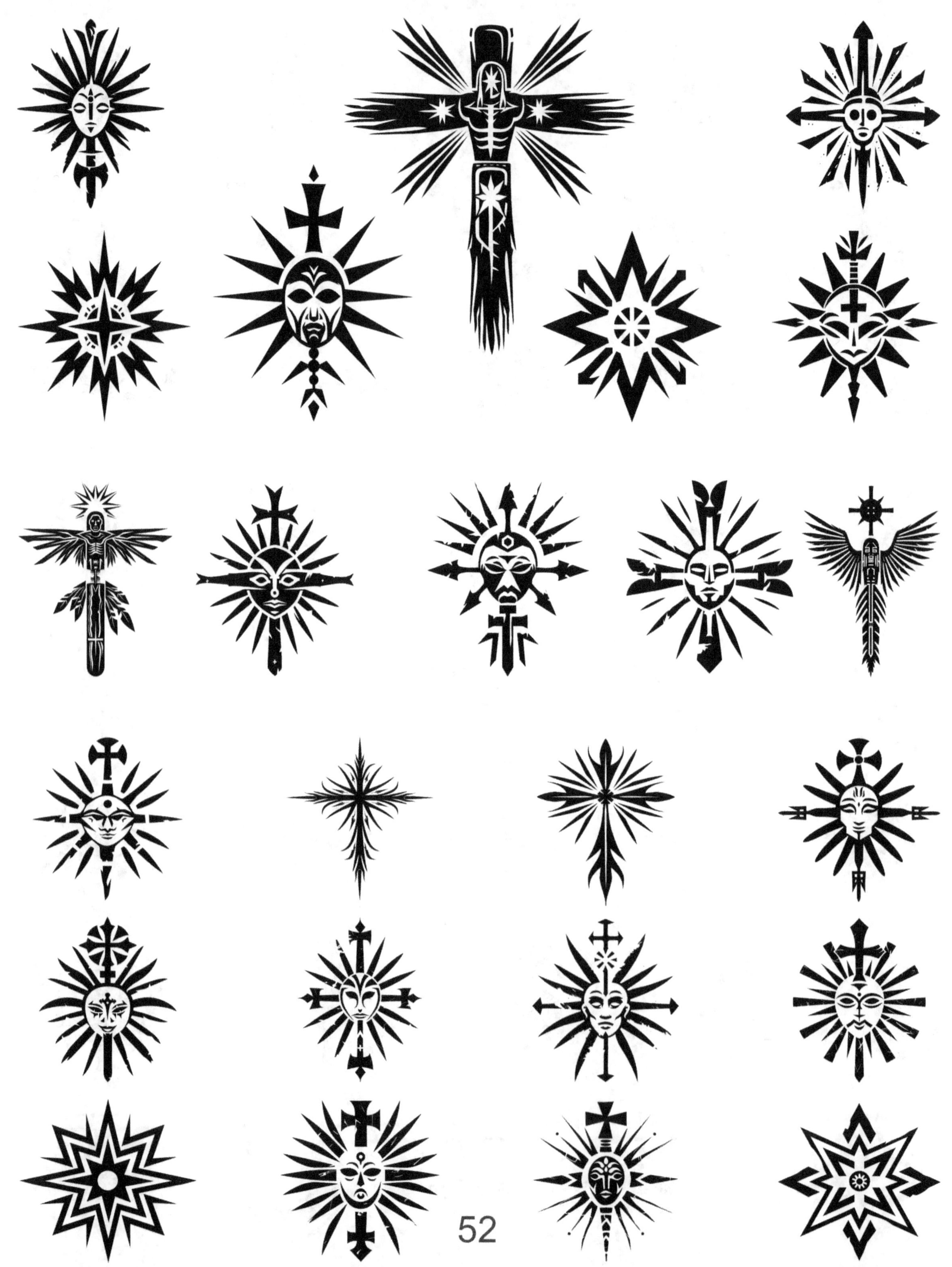

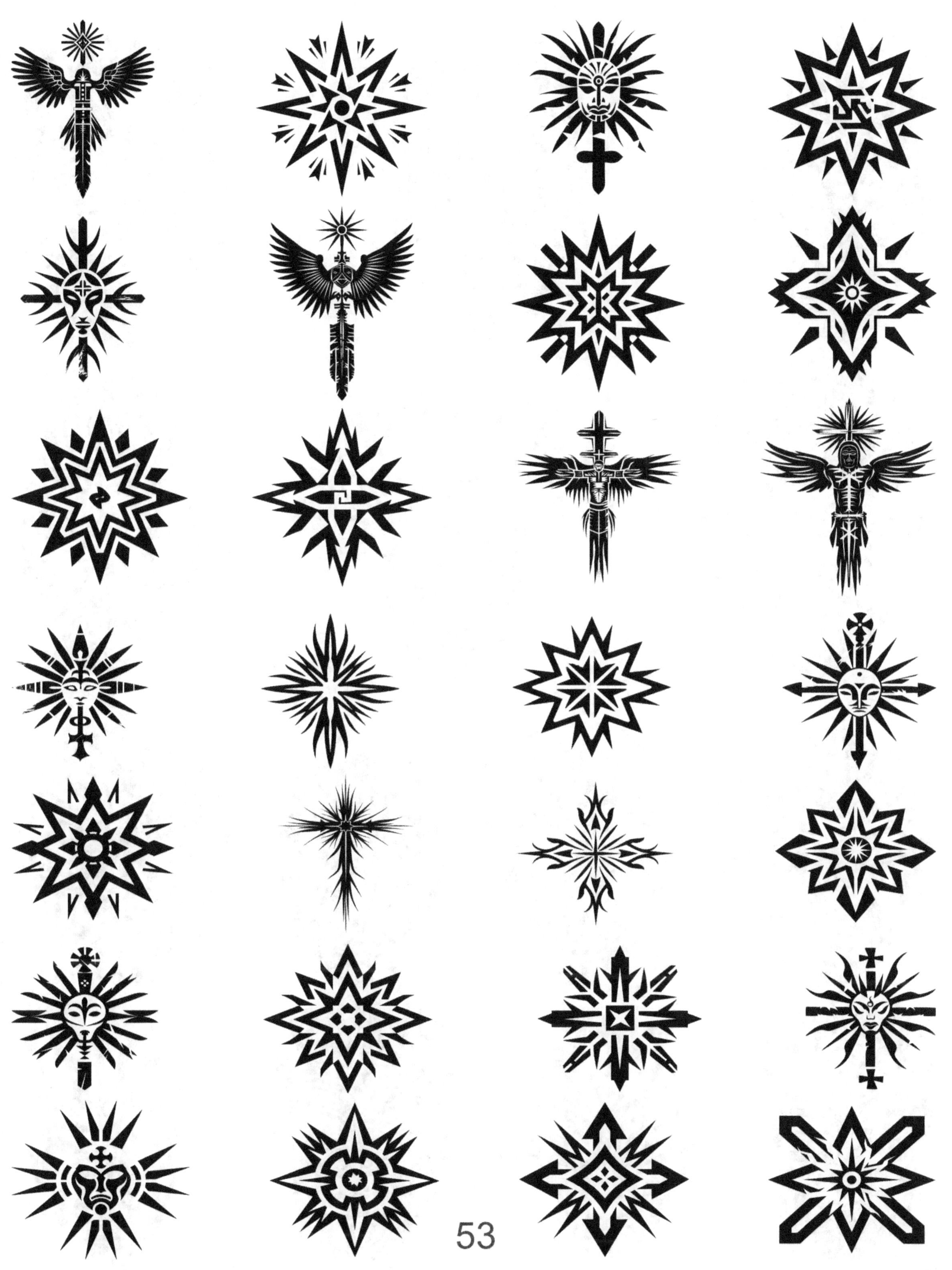

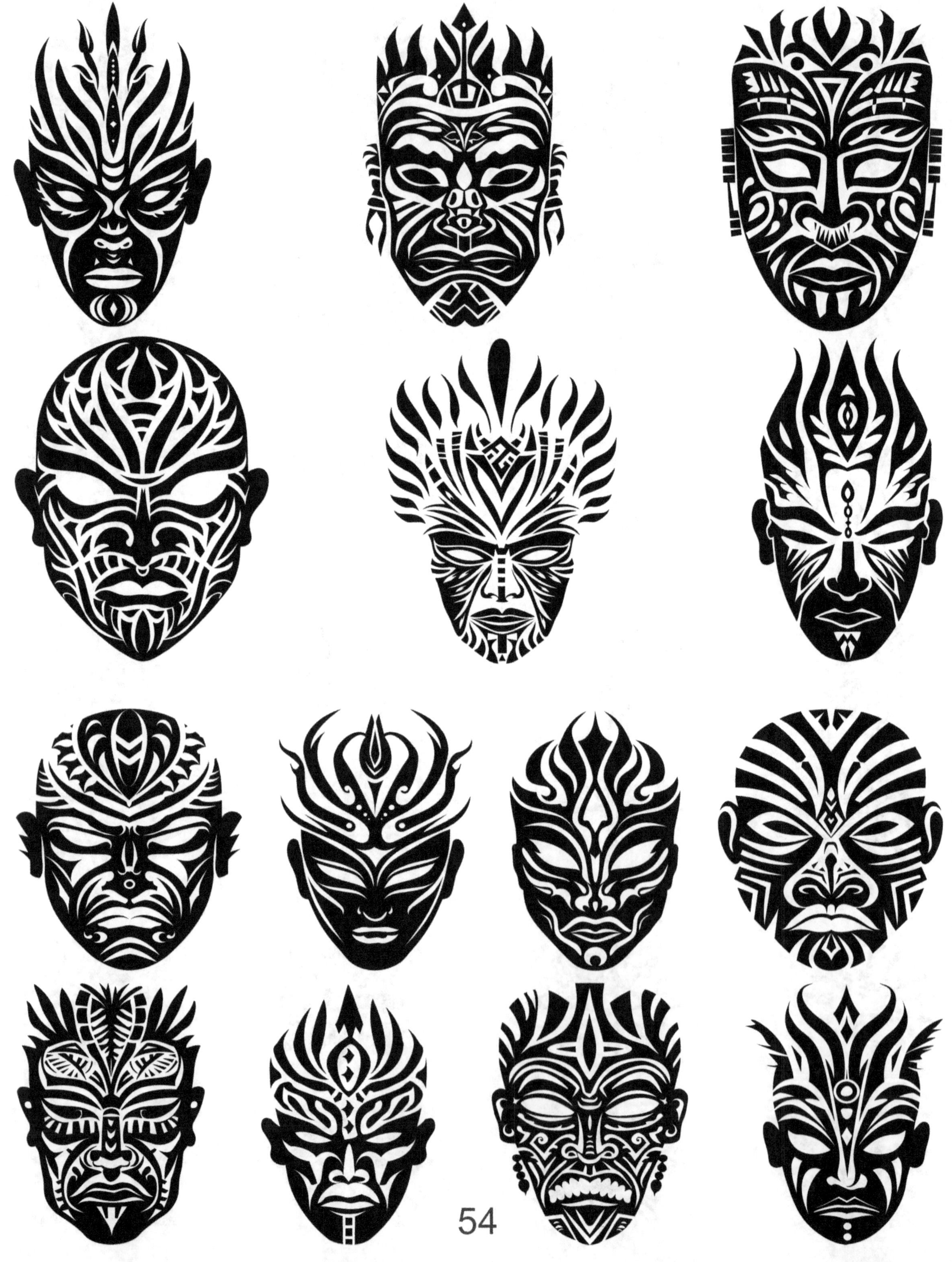

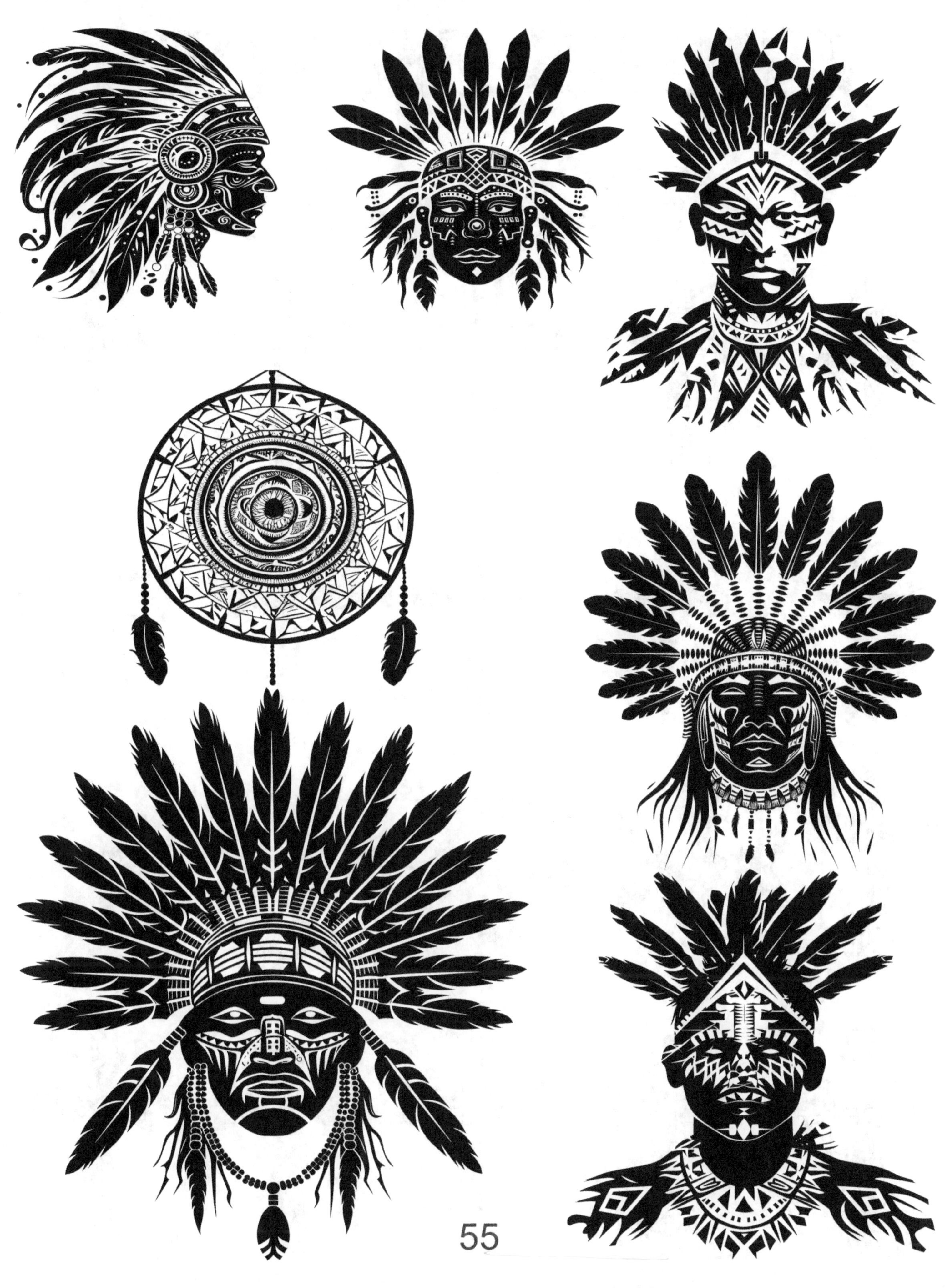

55

CROSS SHAPES TATTOOS

CRAZY TATTOOS

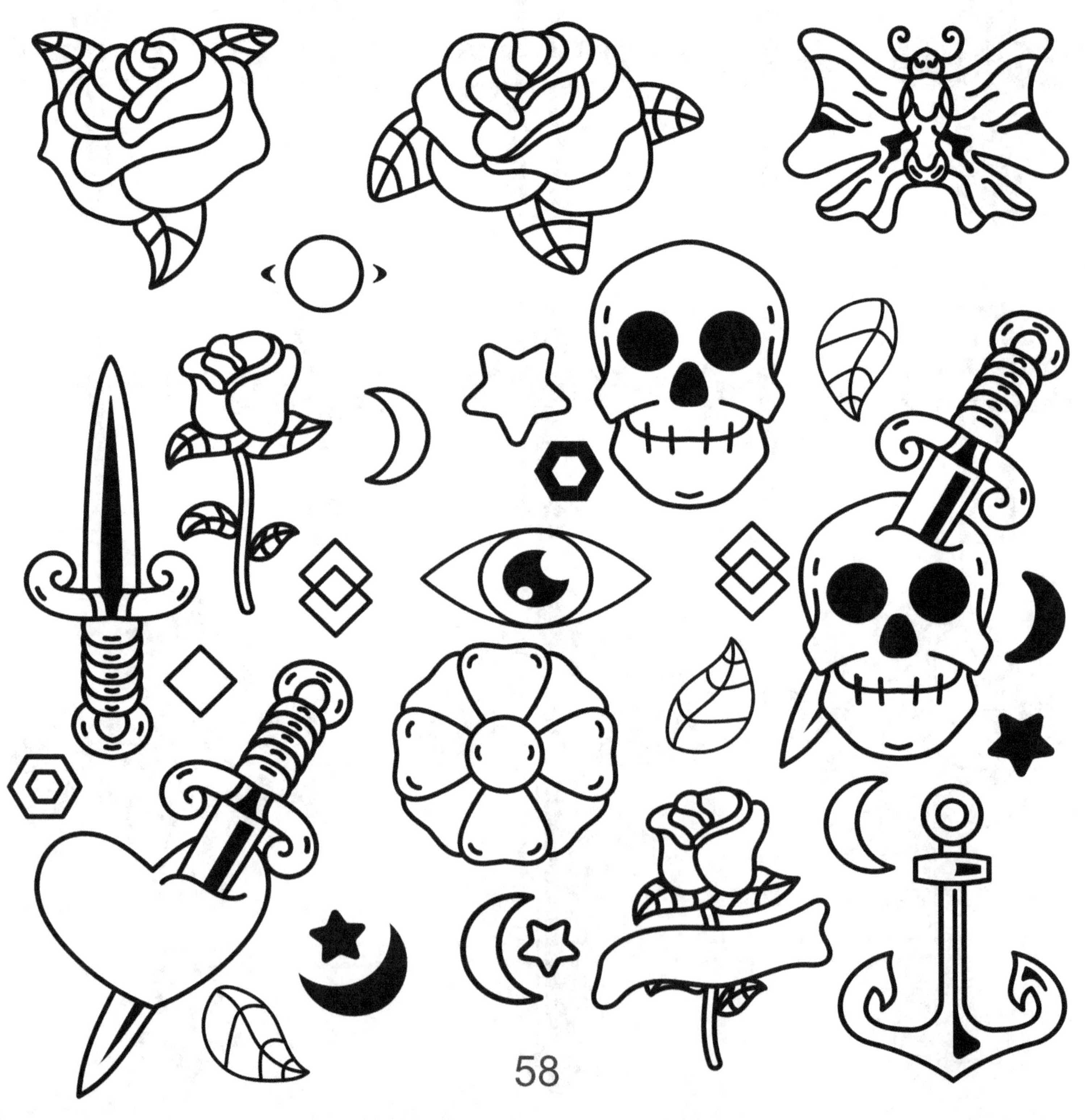

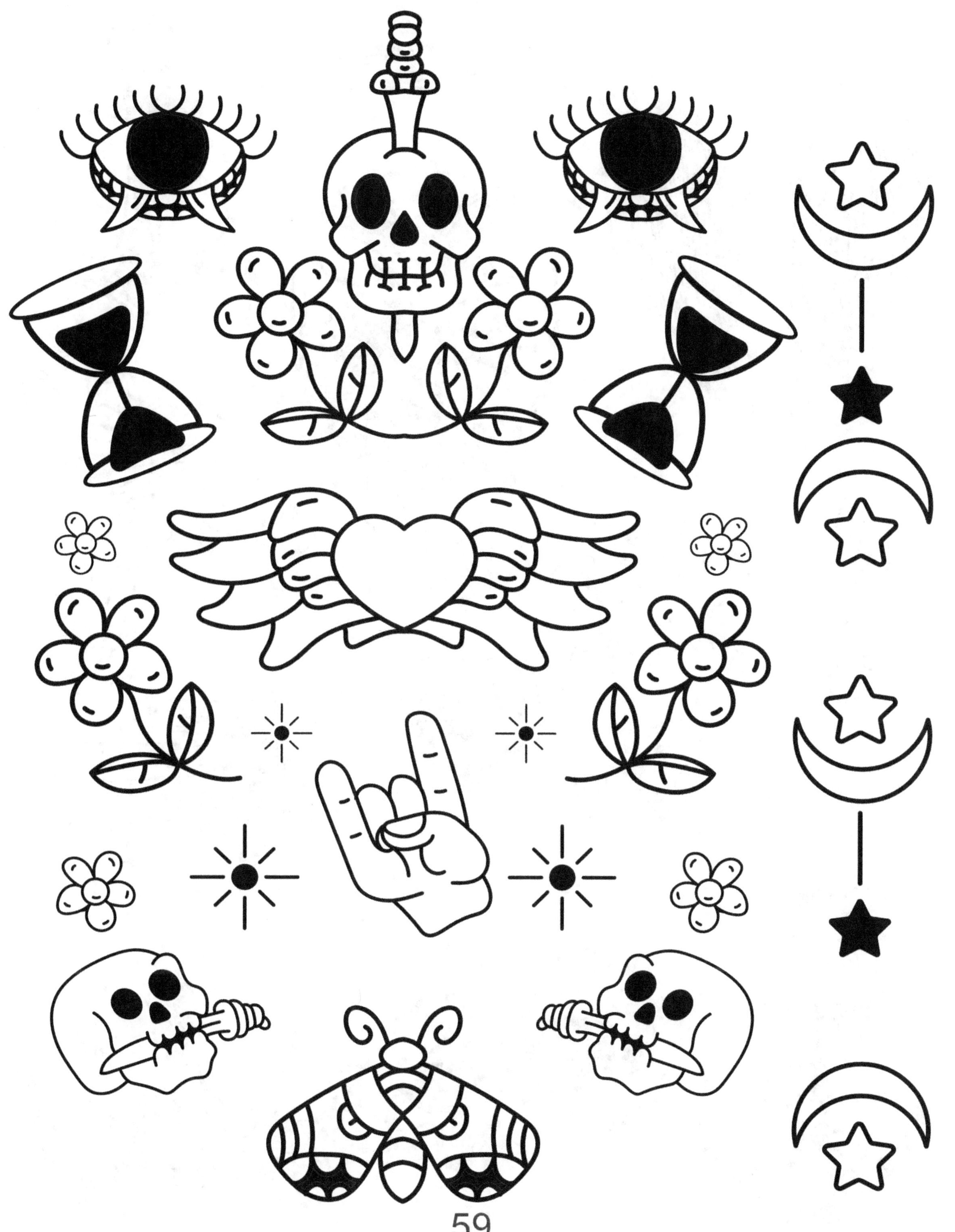

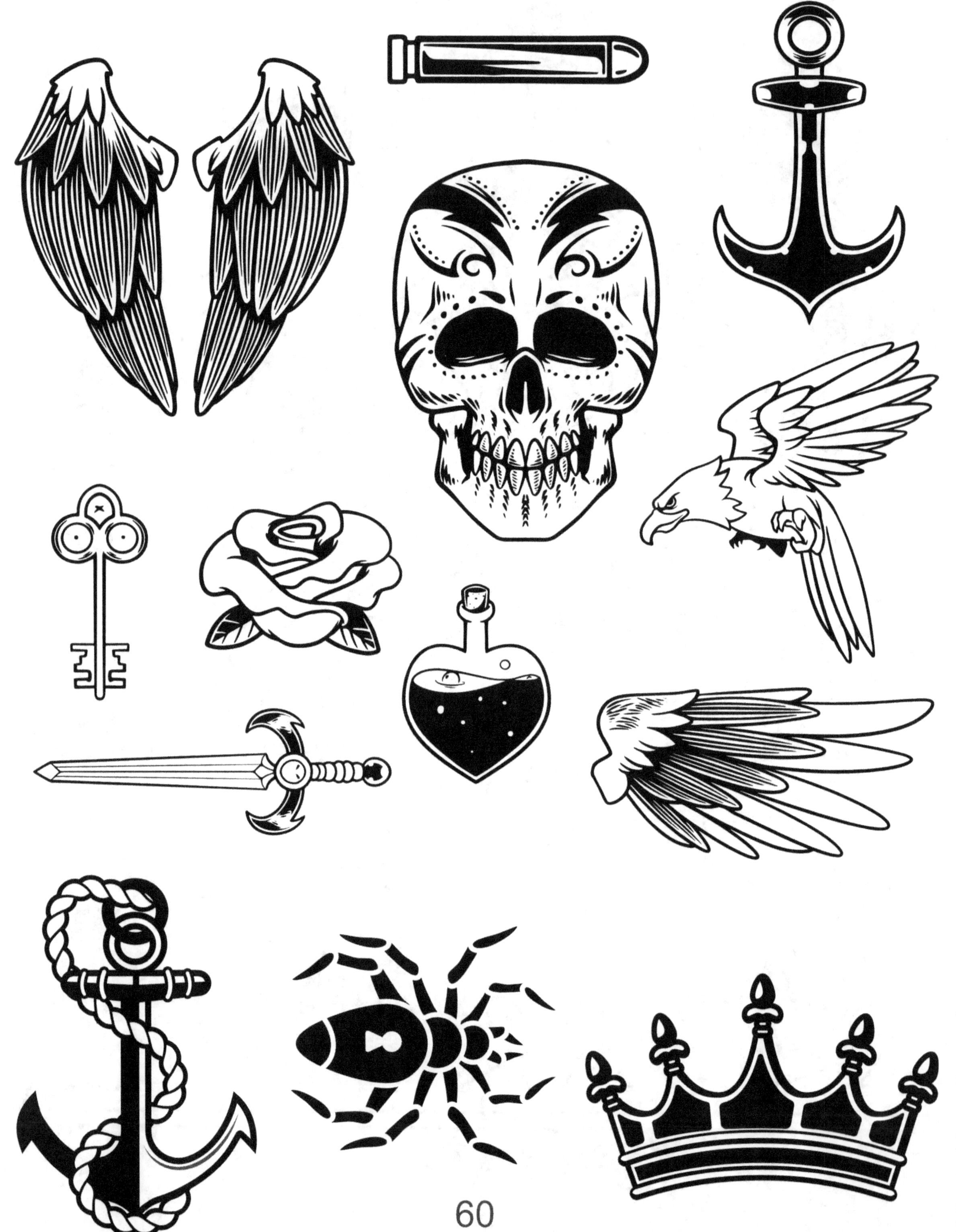

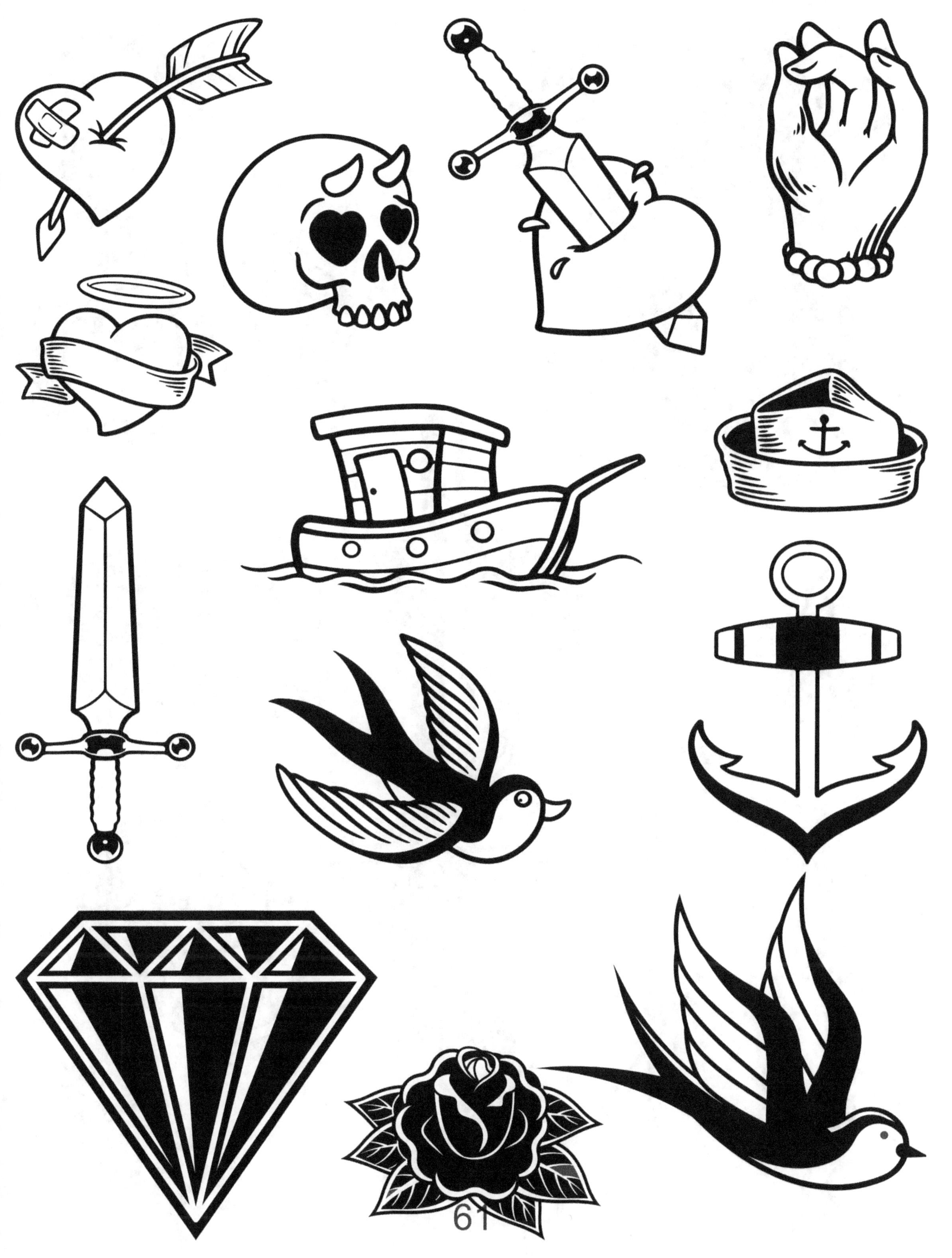

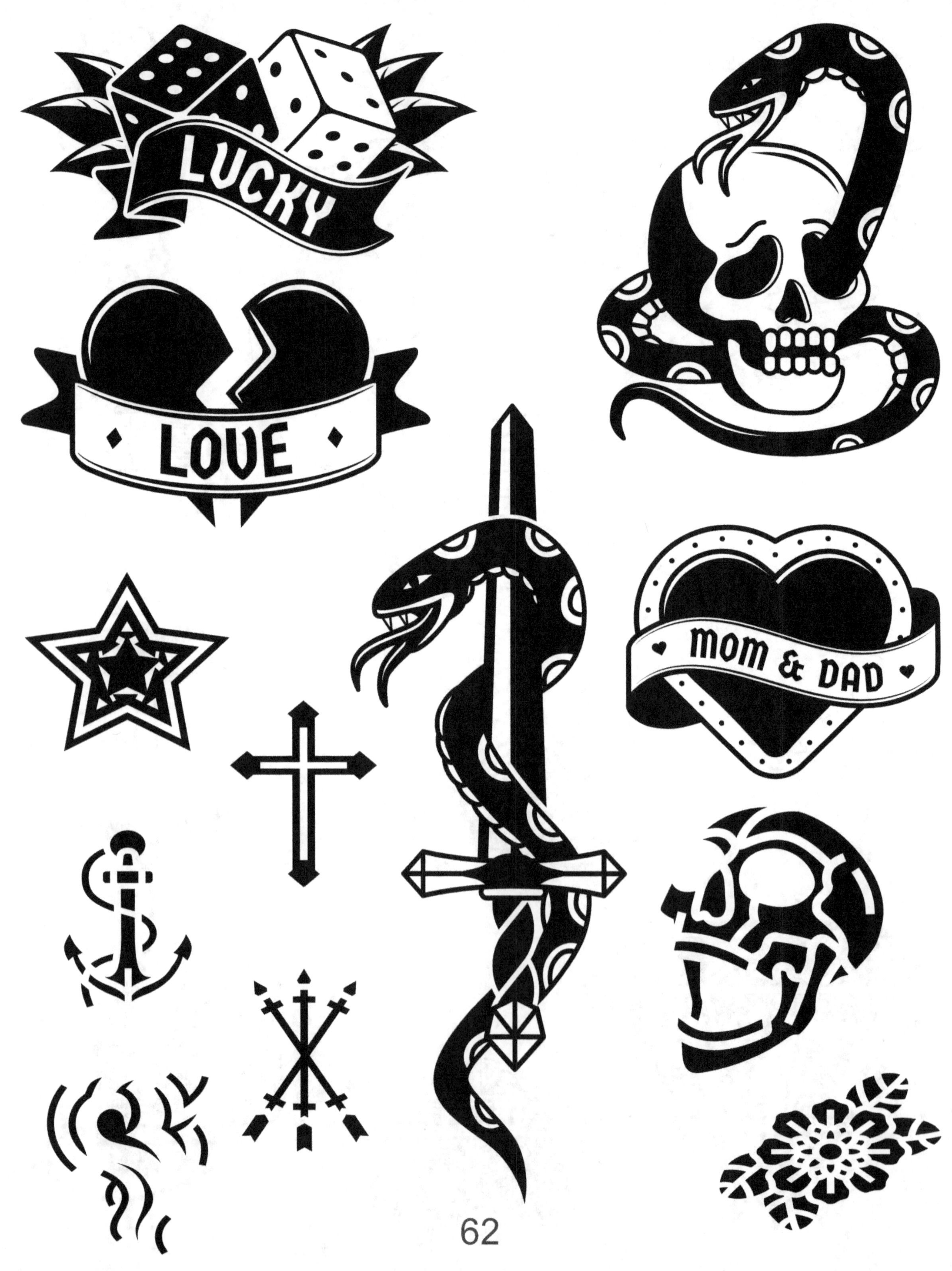

LUCKY
LOVE
mom & DAD

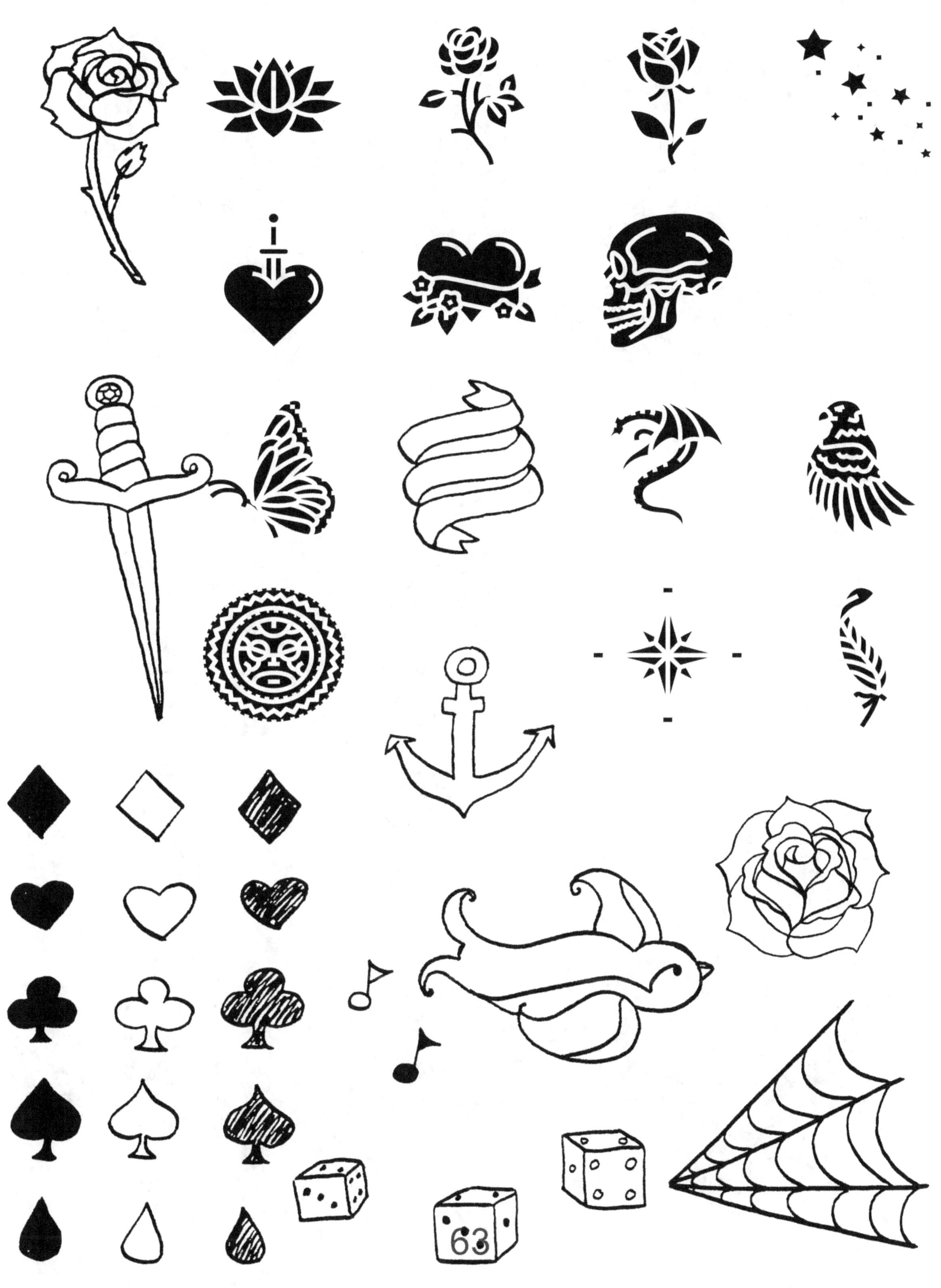

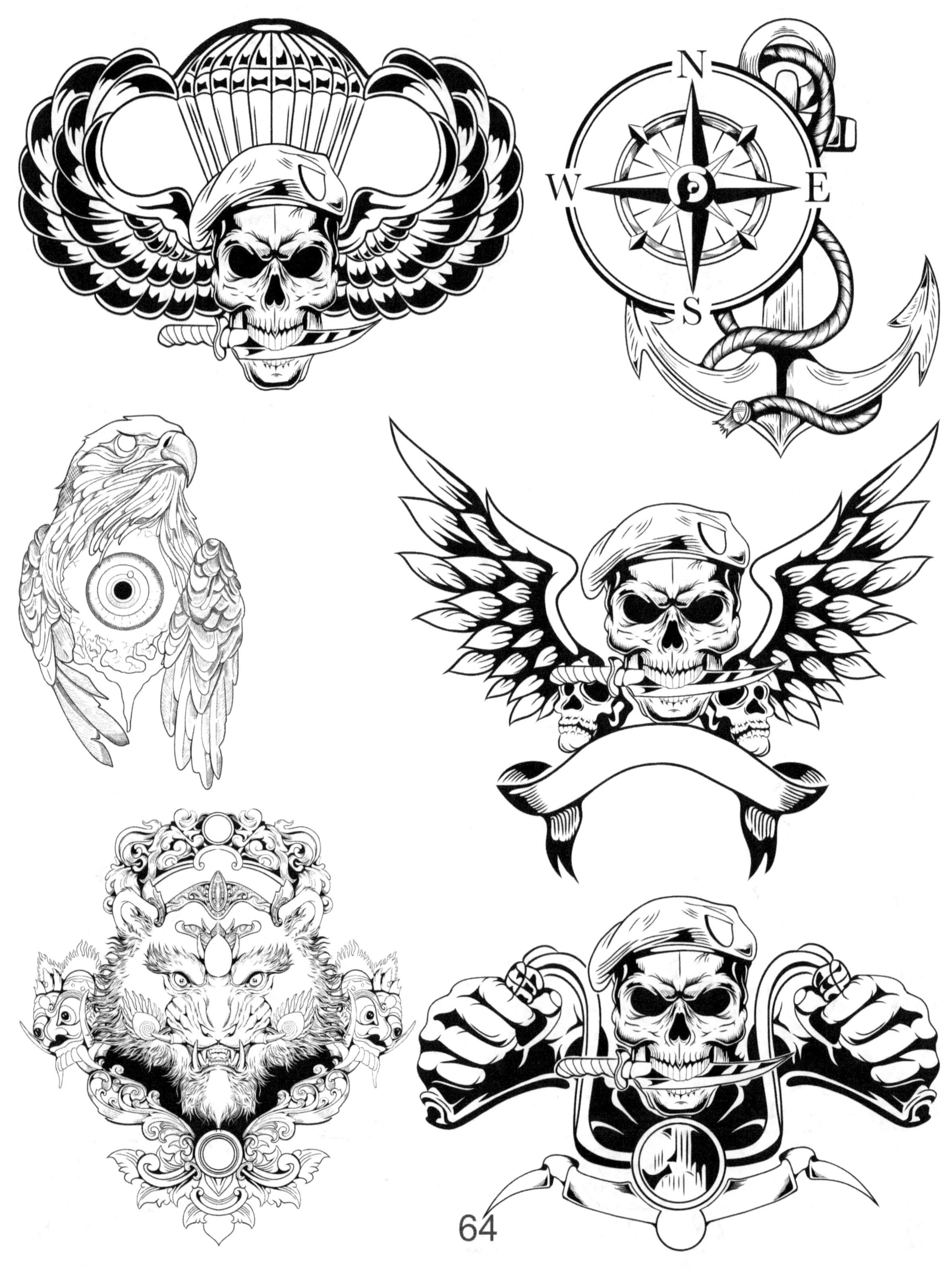

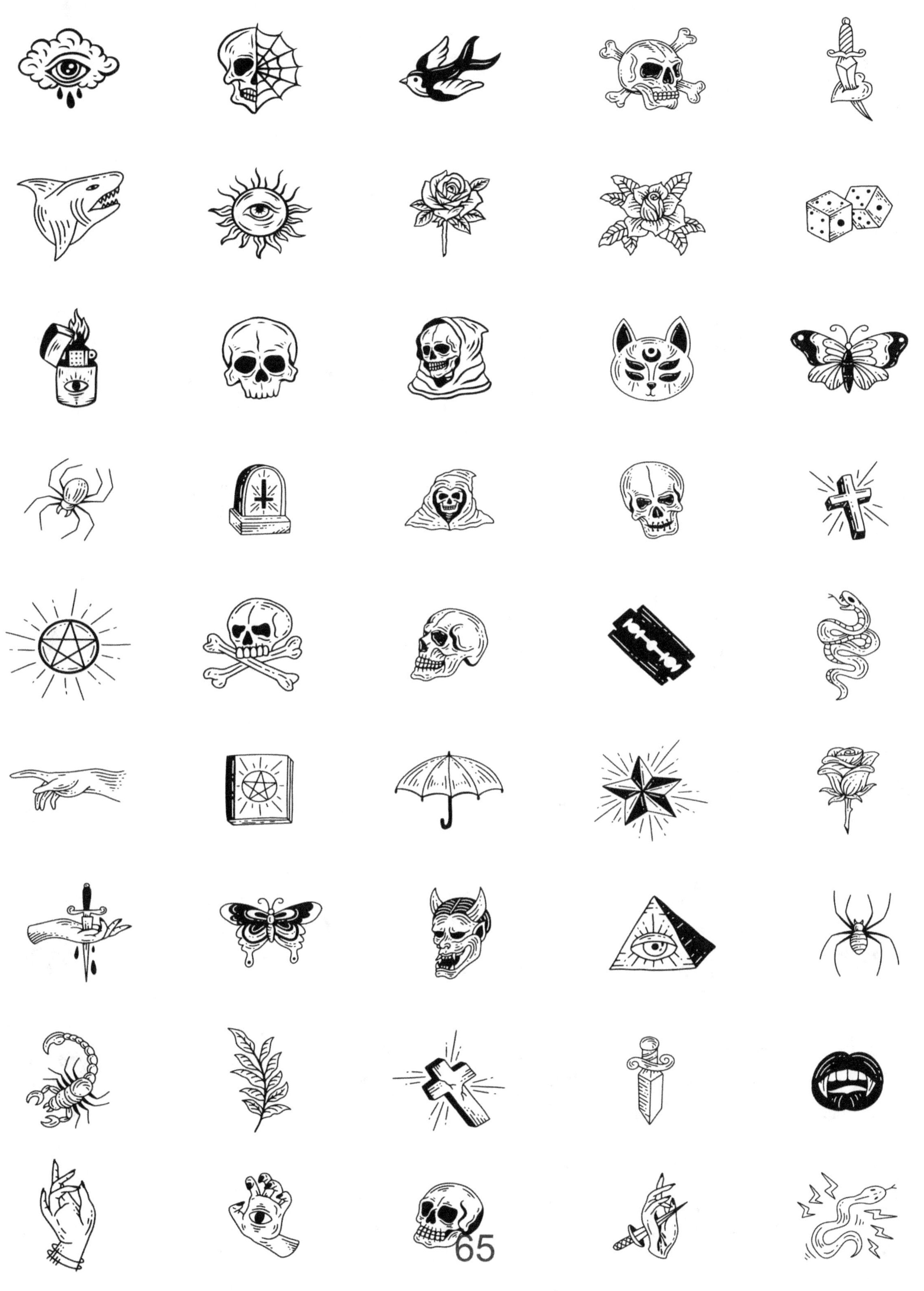

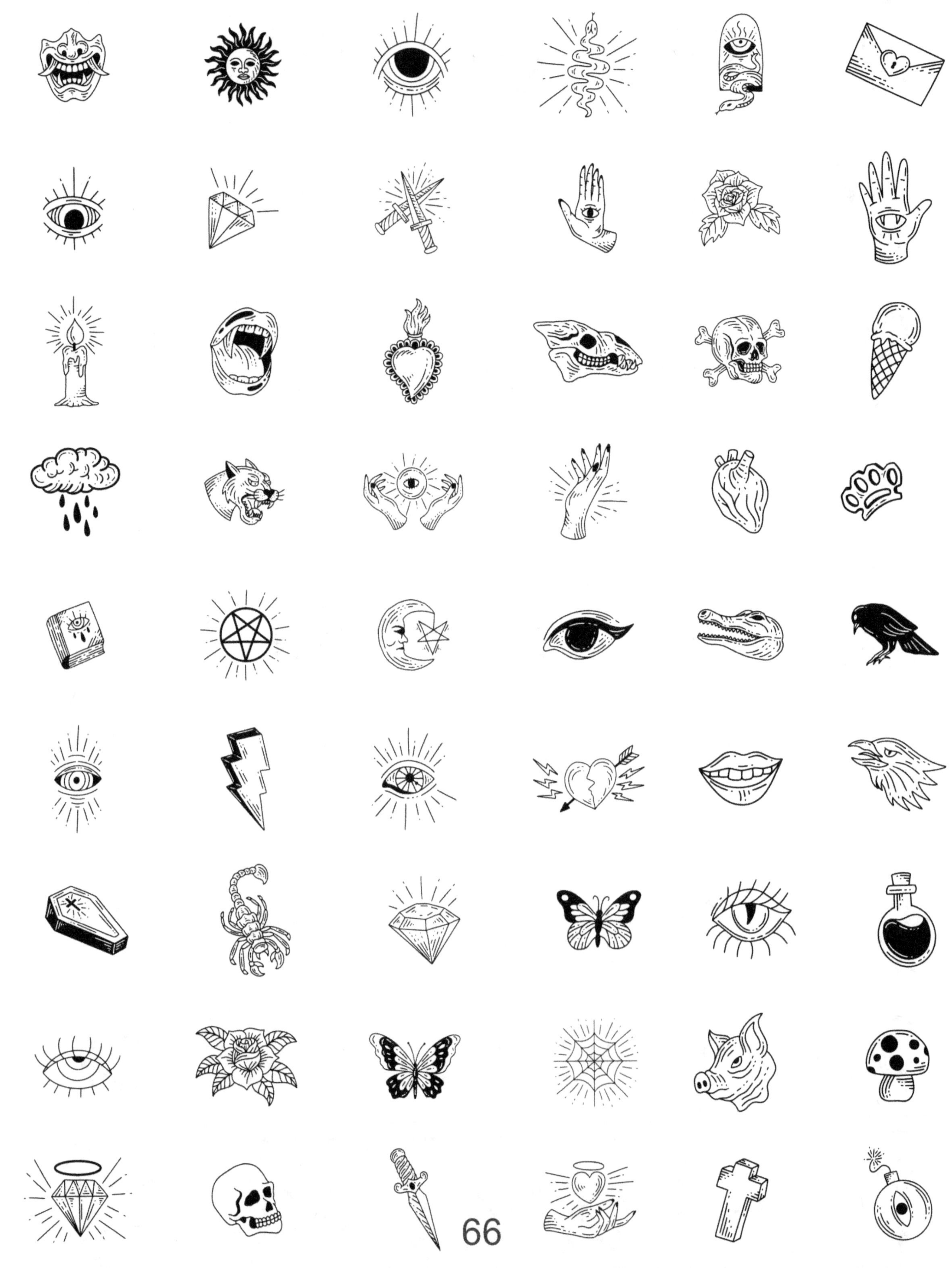

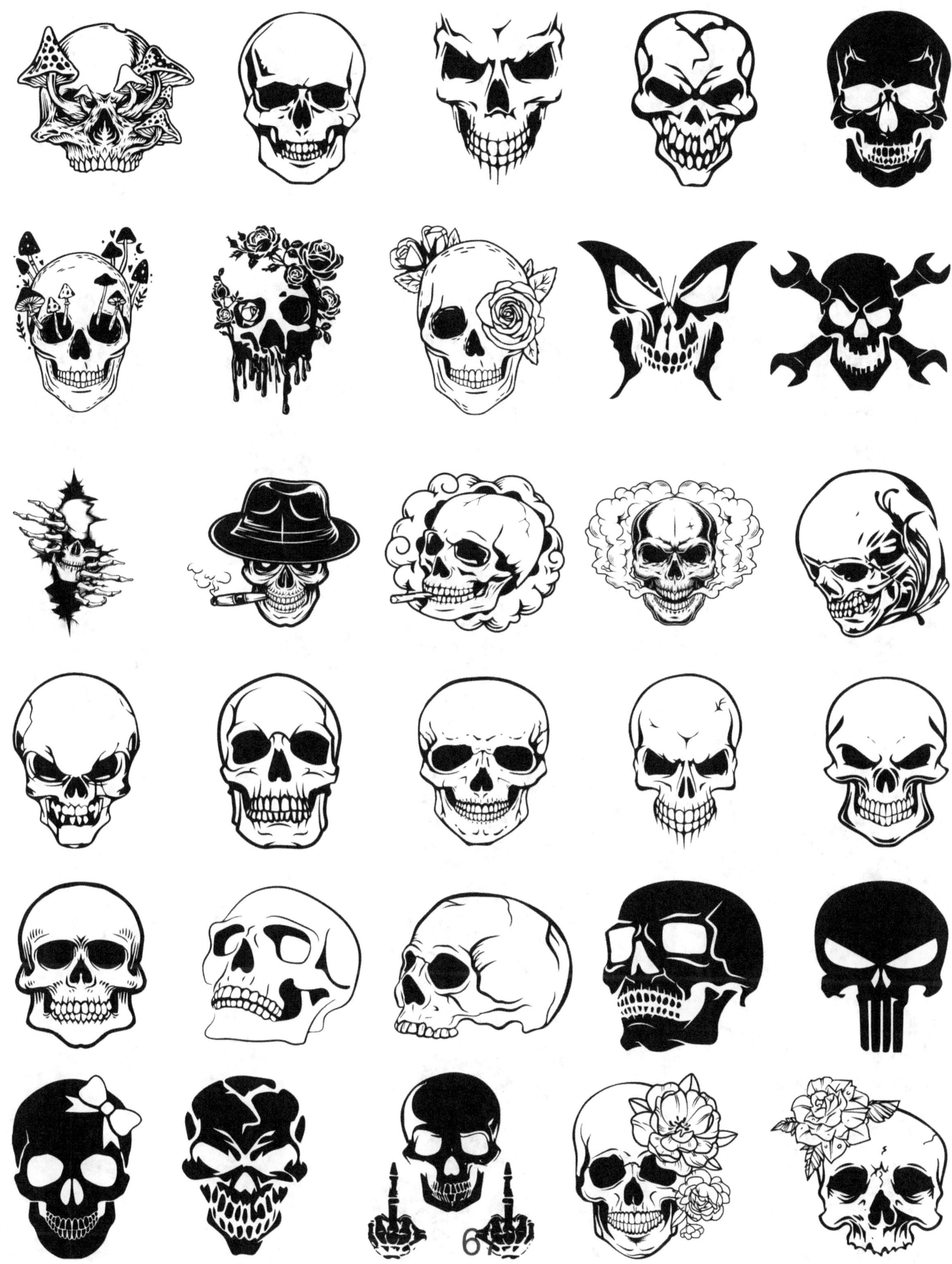

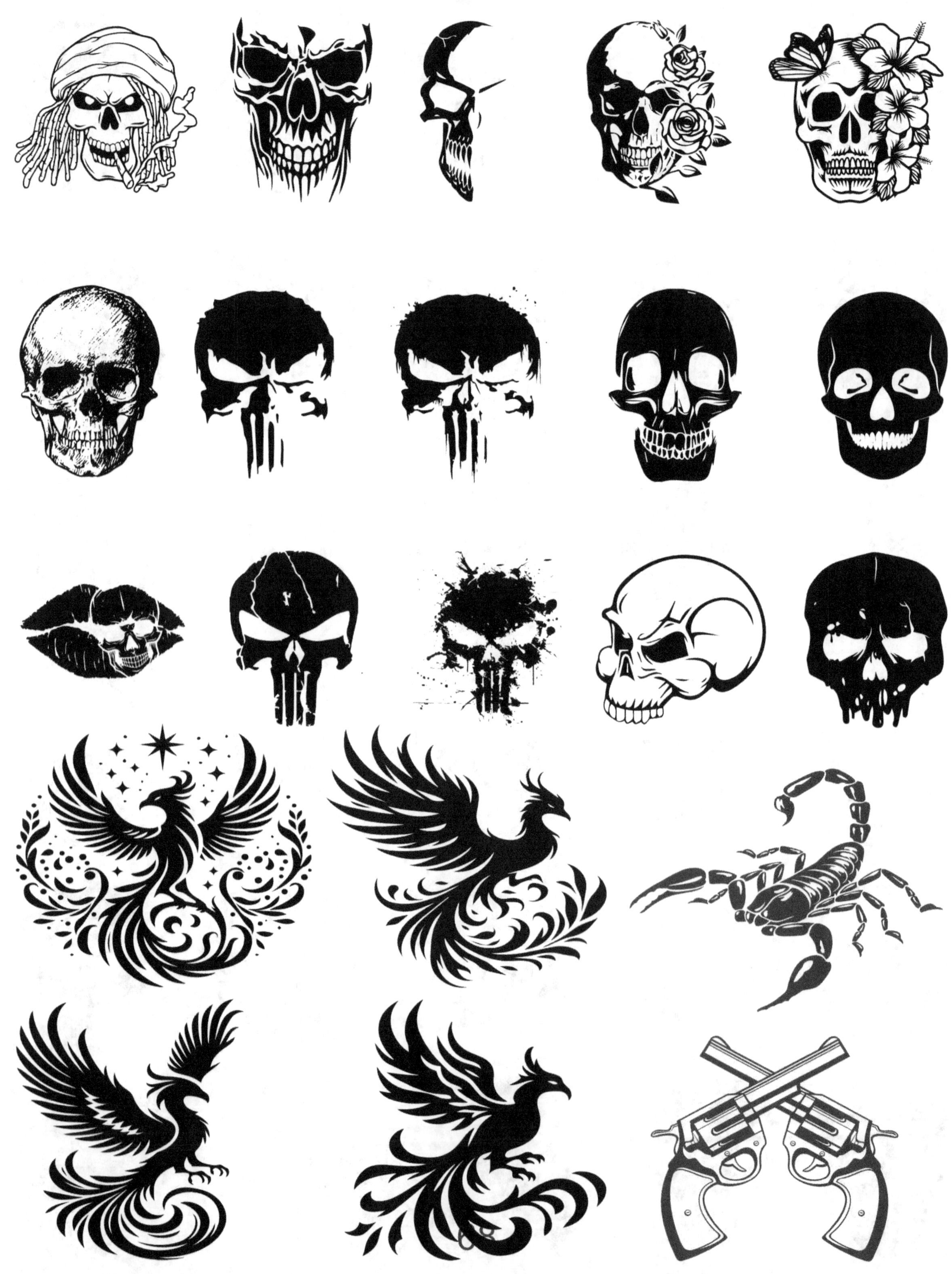

FLORAL TATTOOS

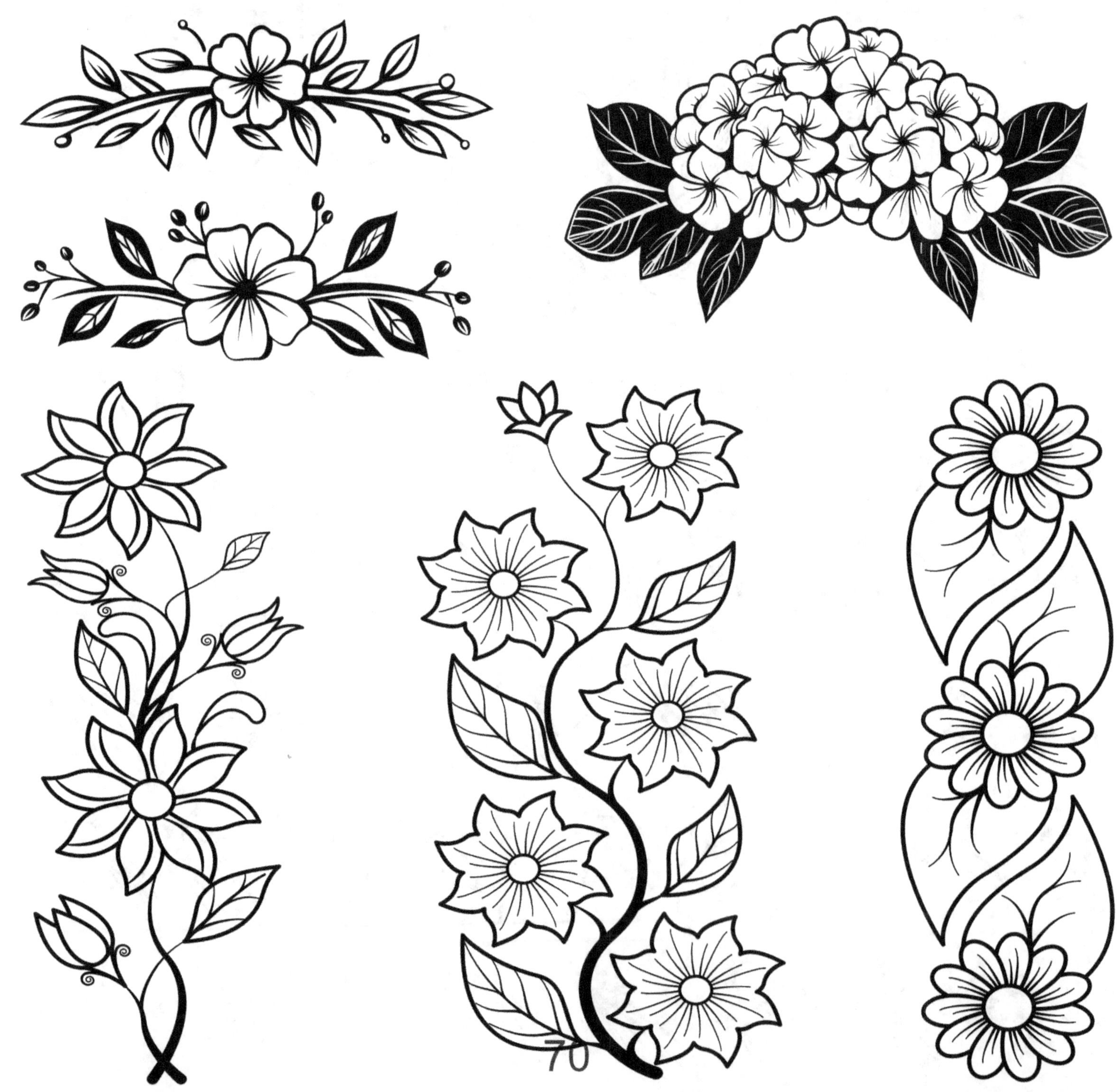

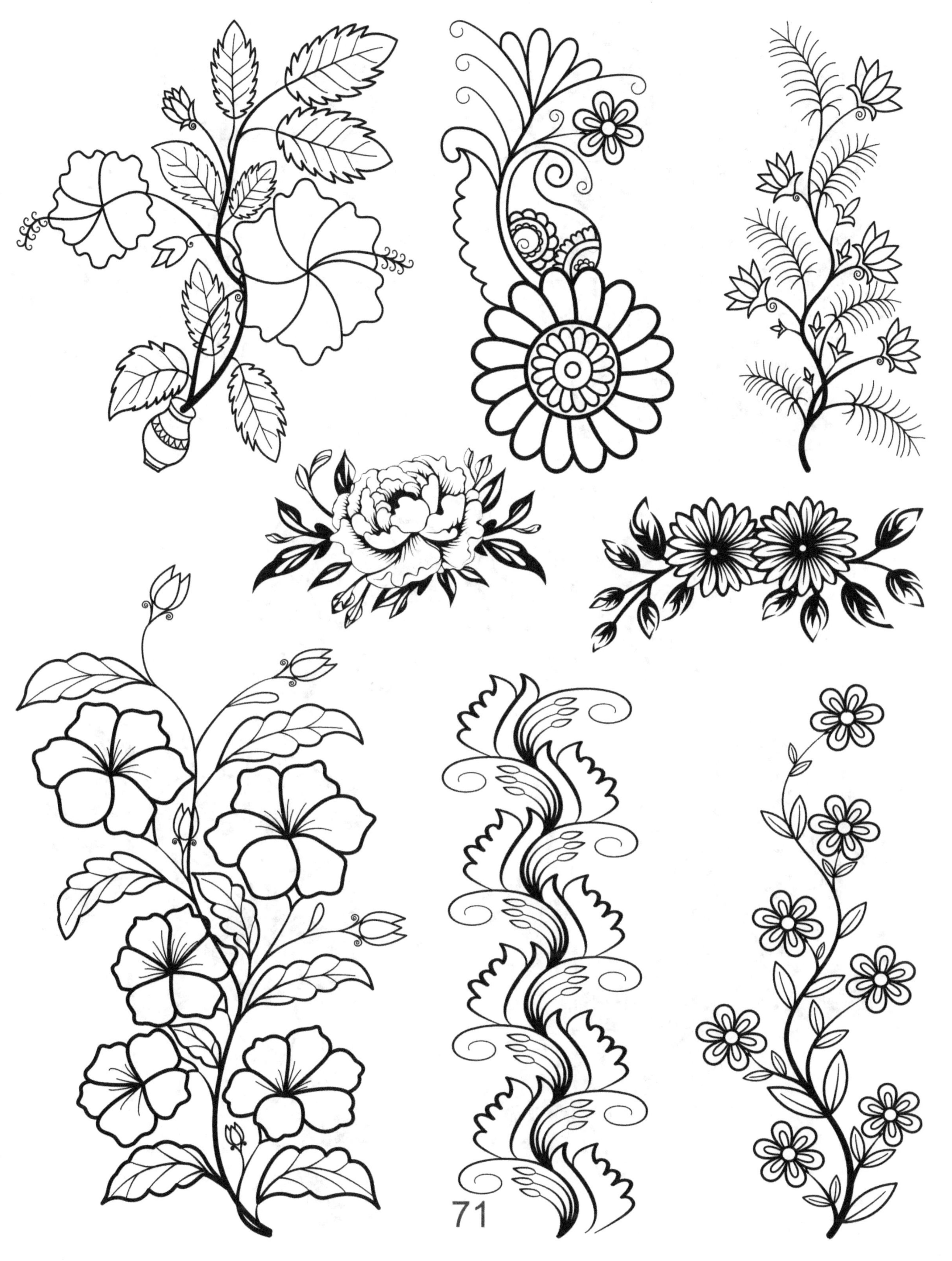

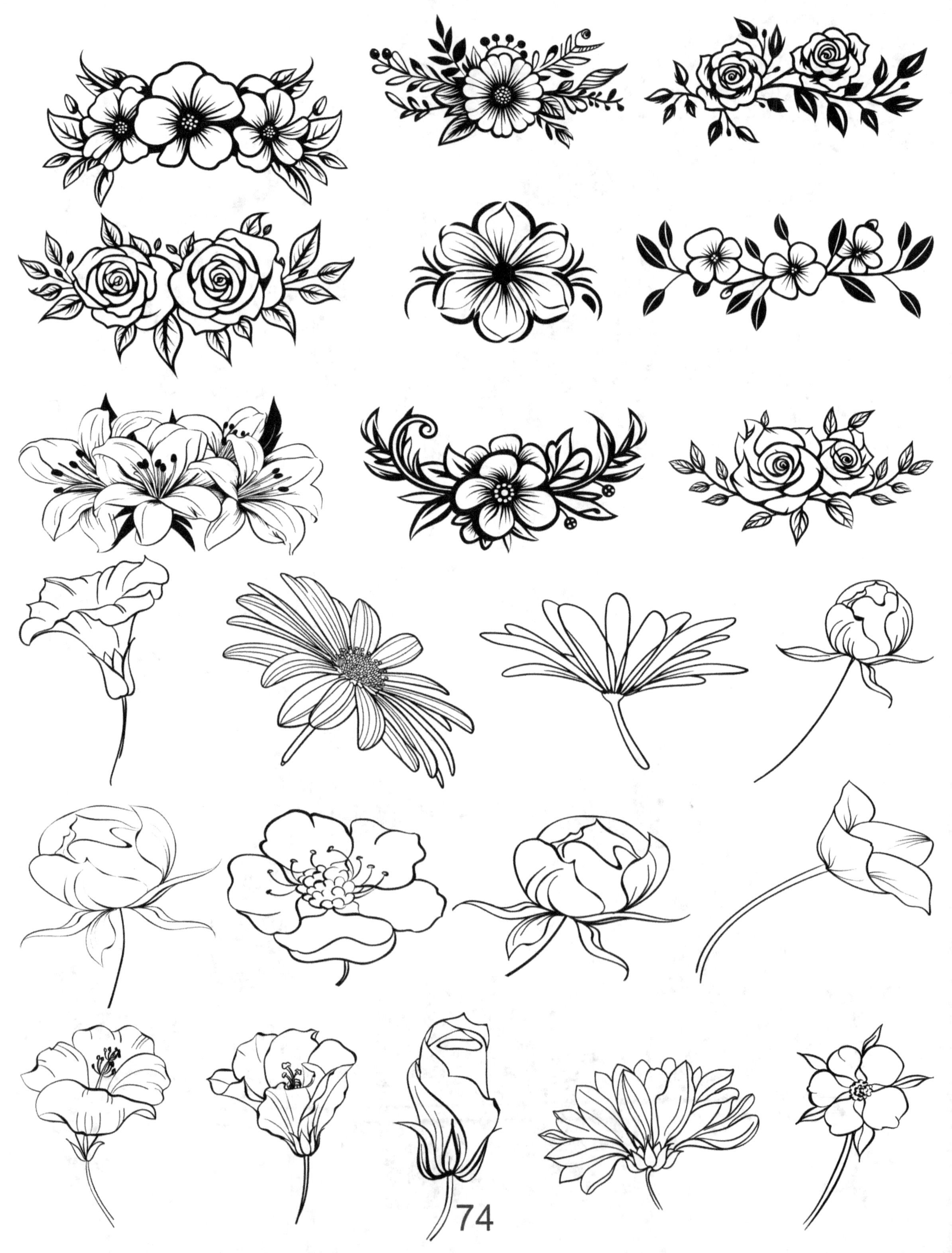

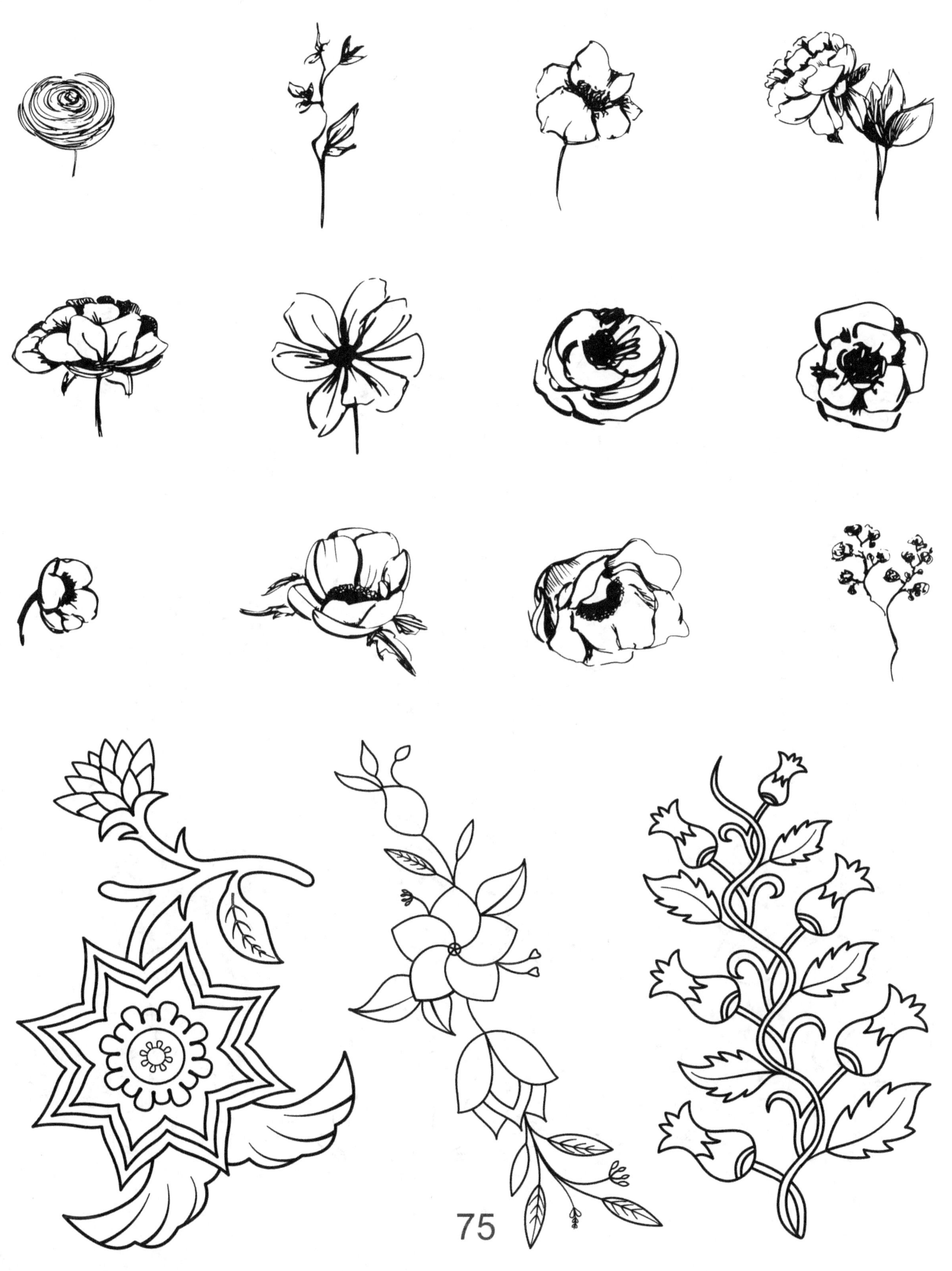

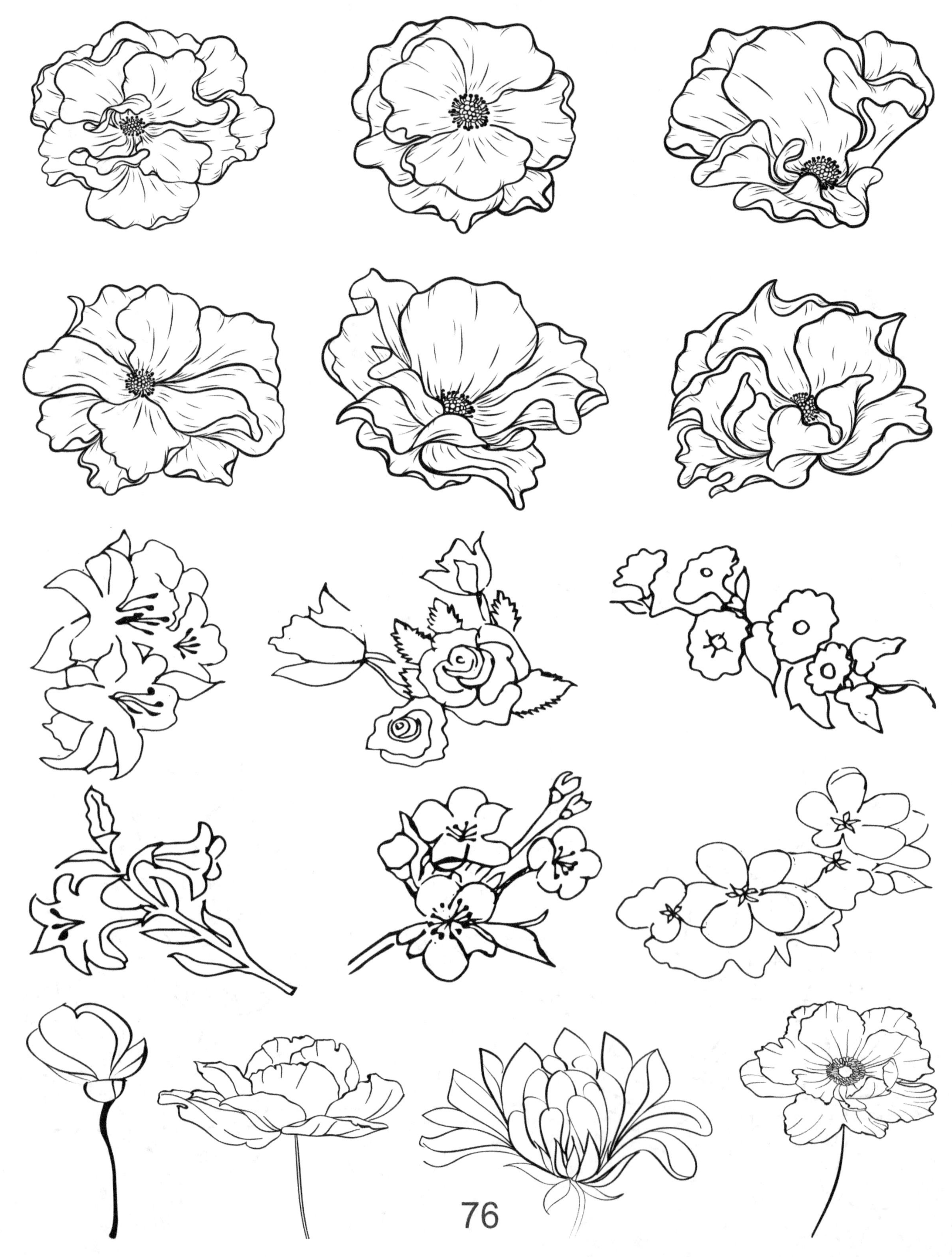

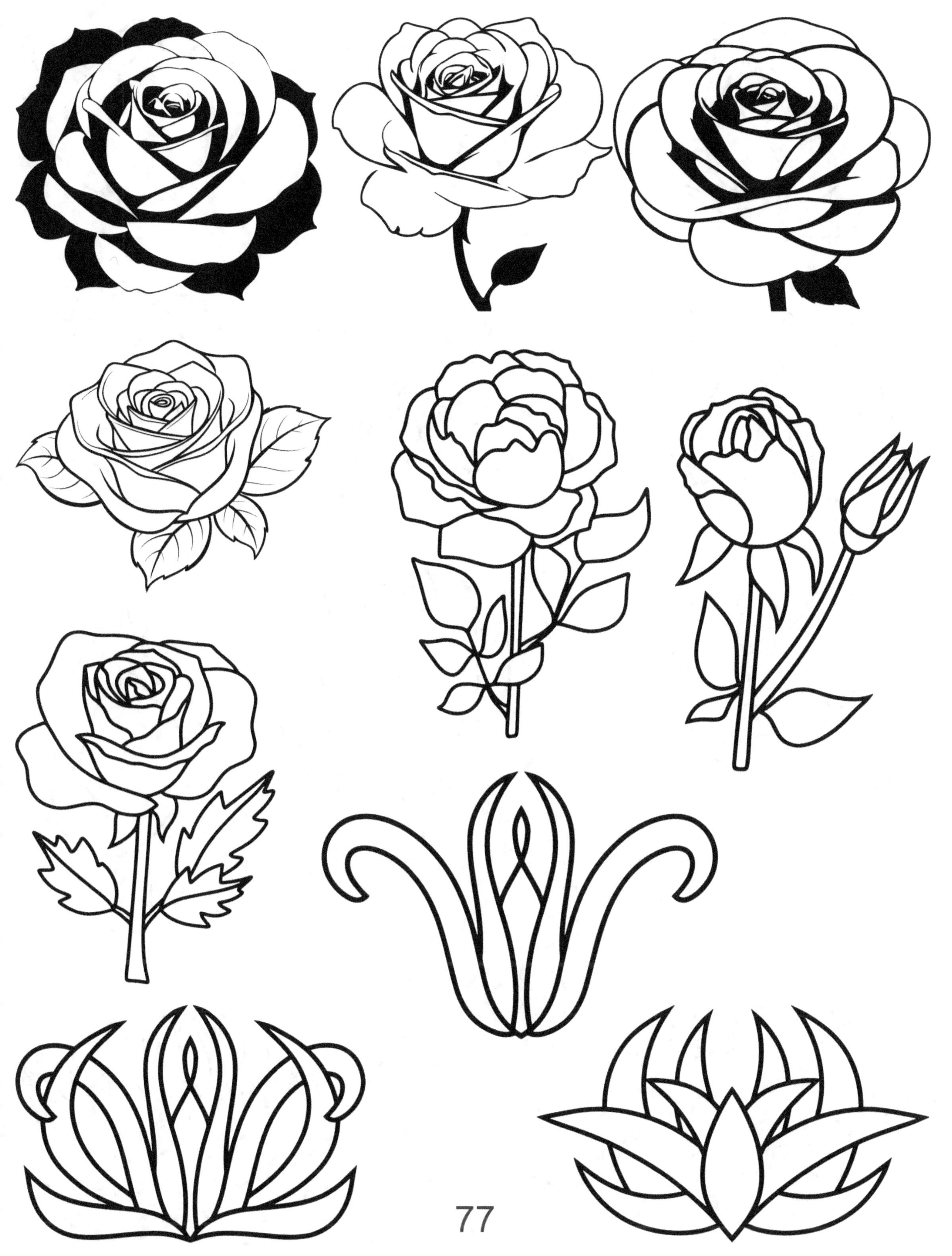

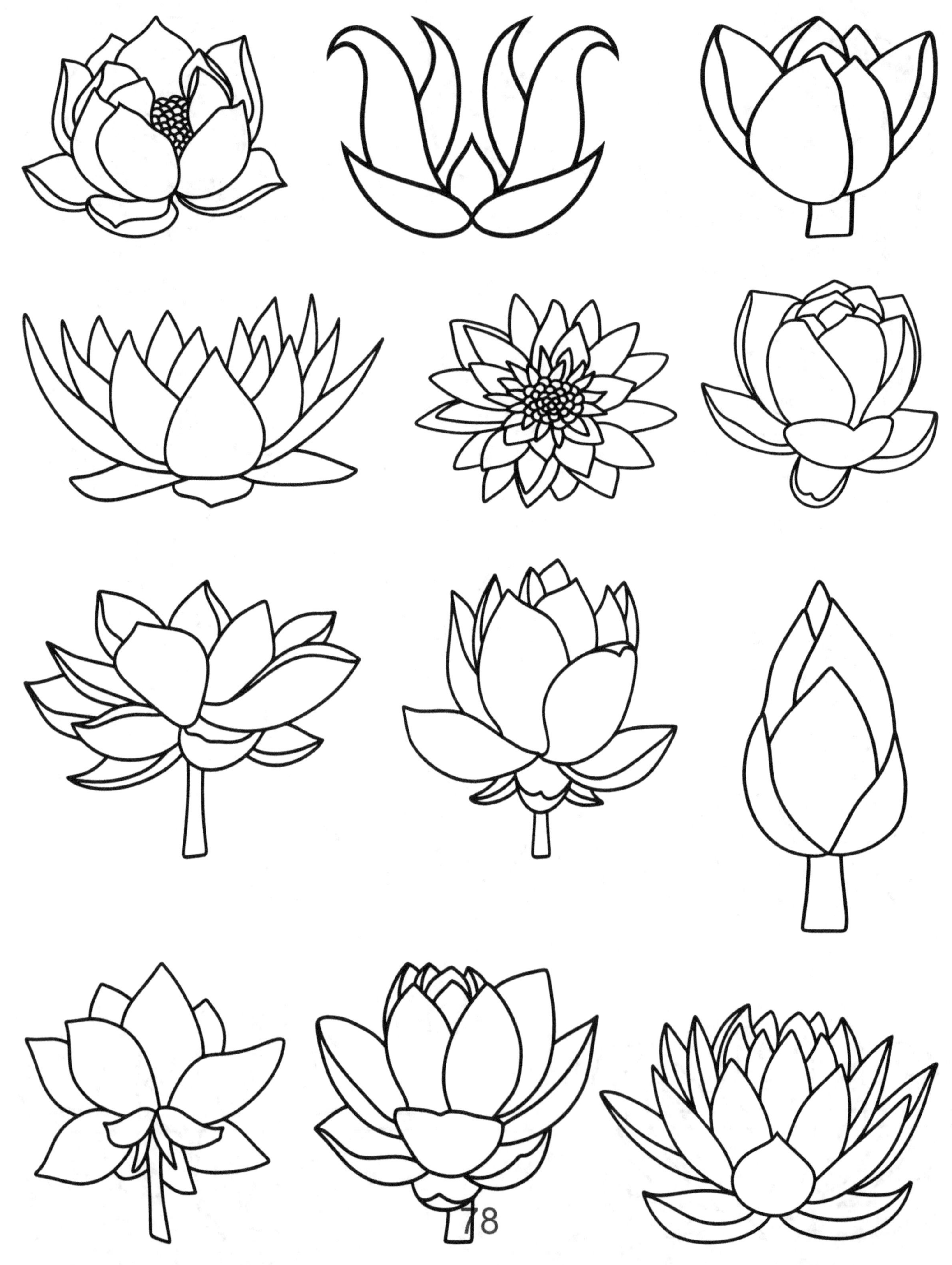

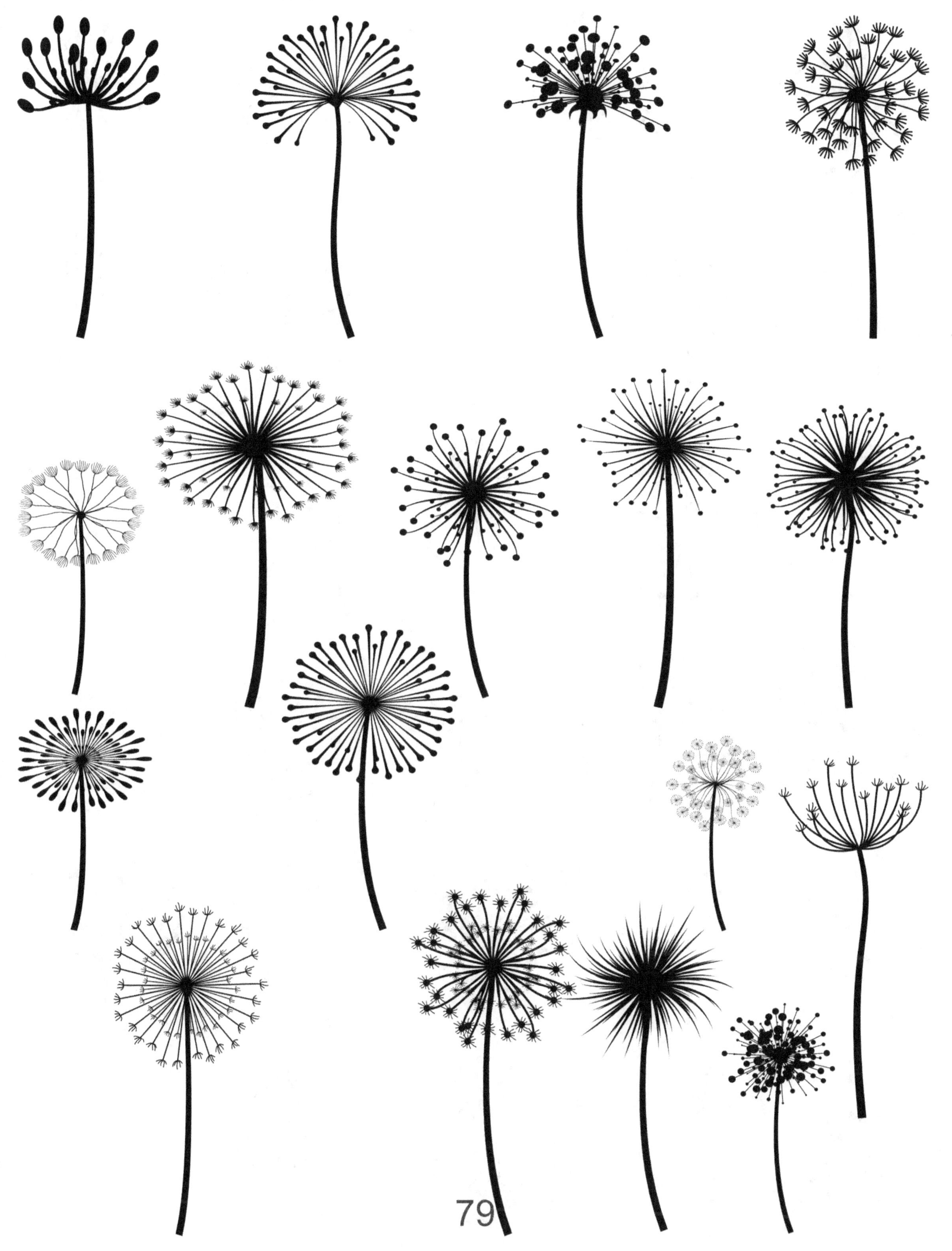

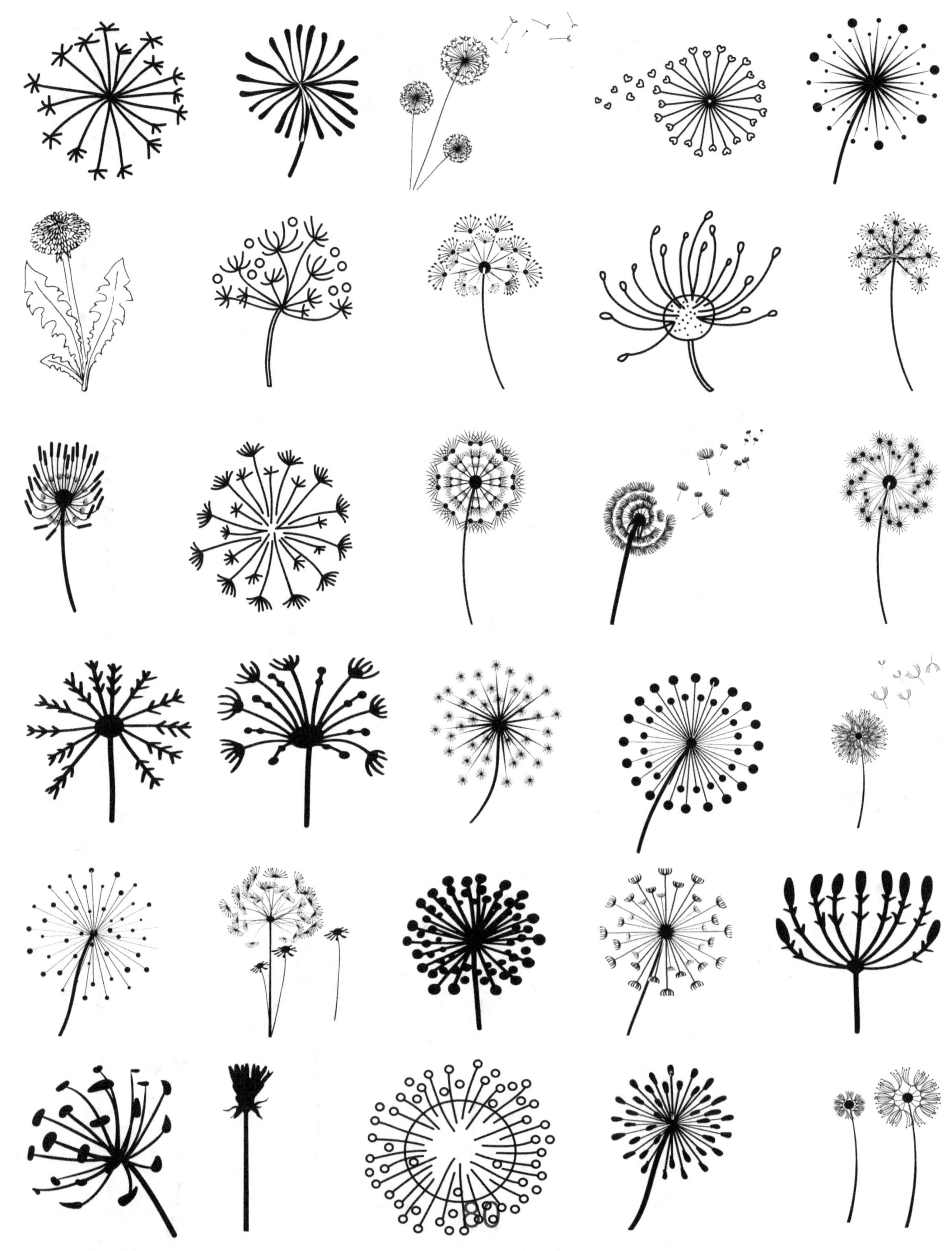

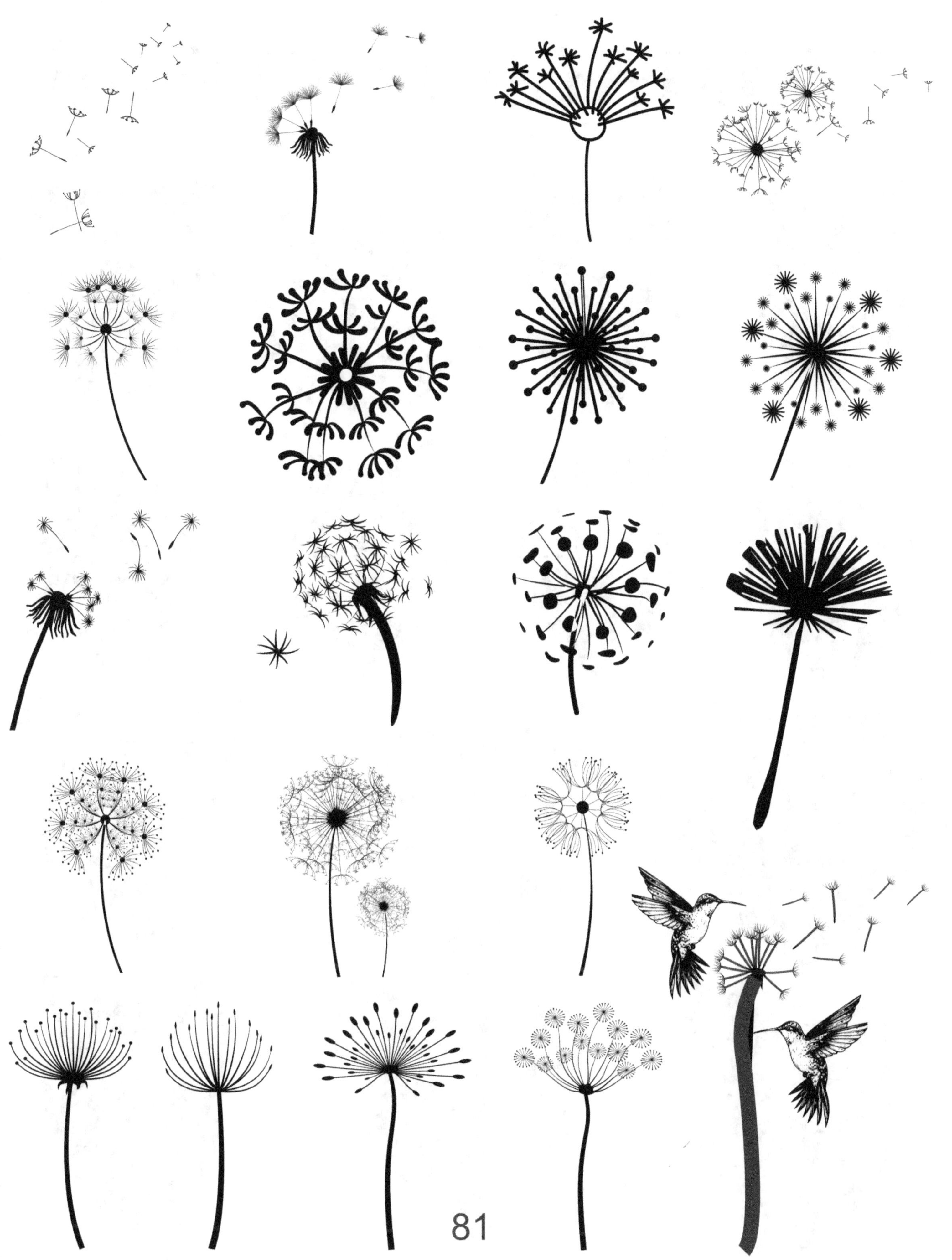

ANIMALS TATTOOS

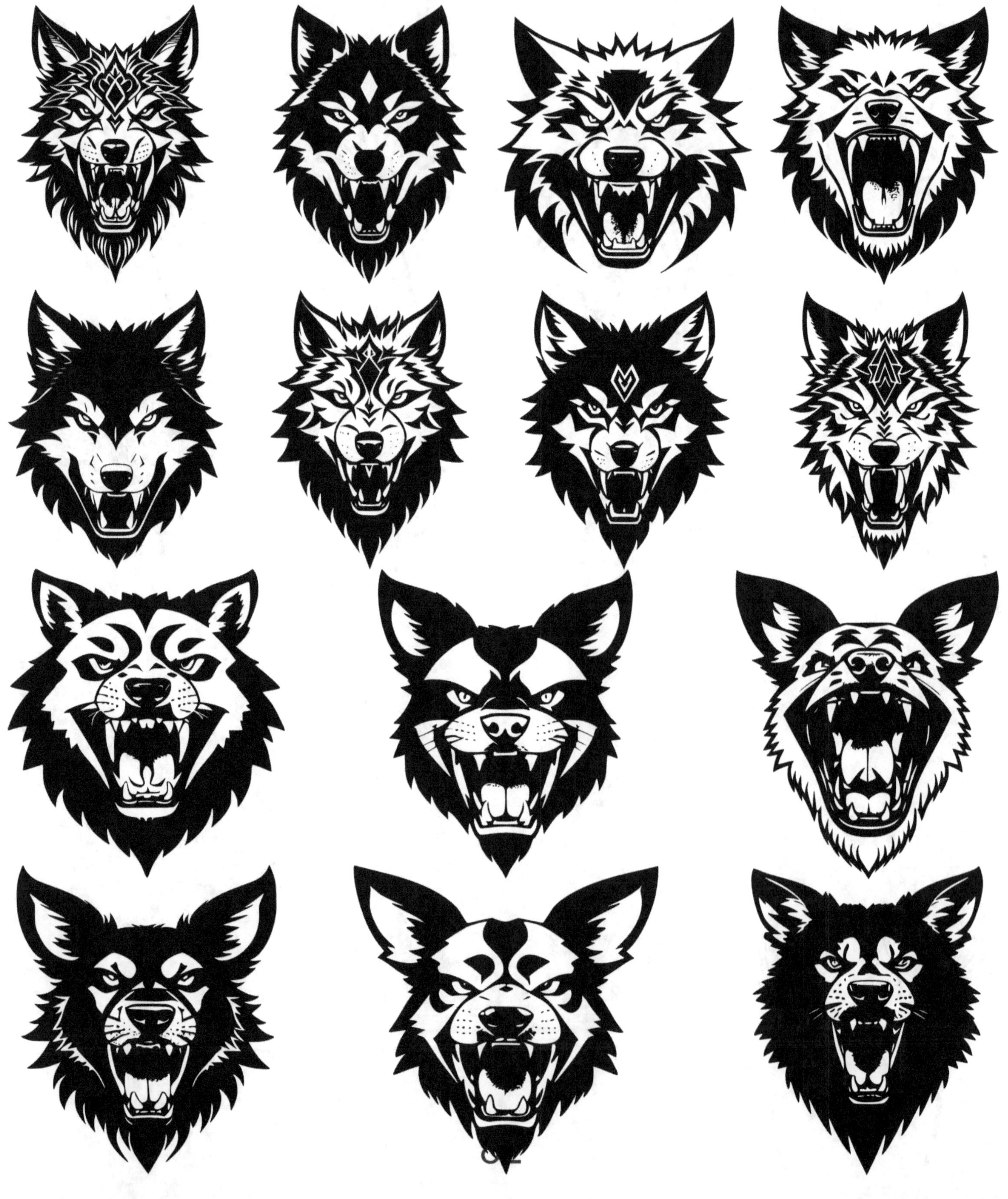

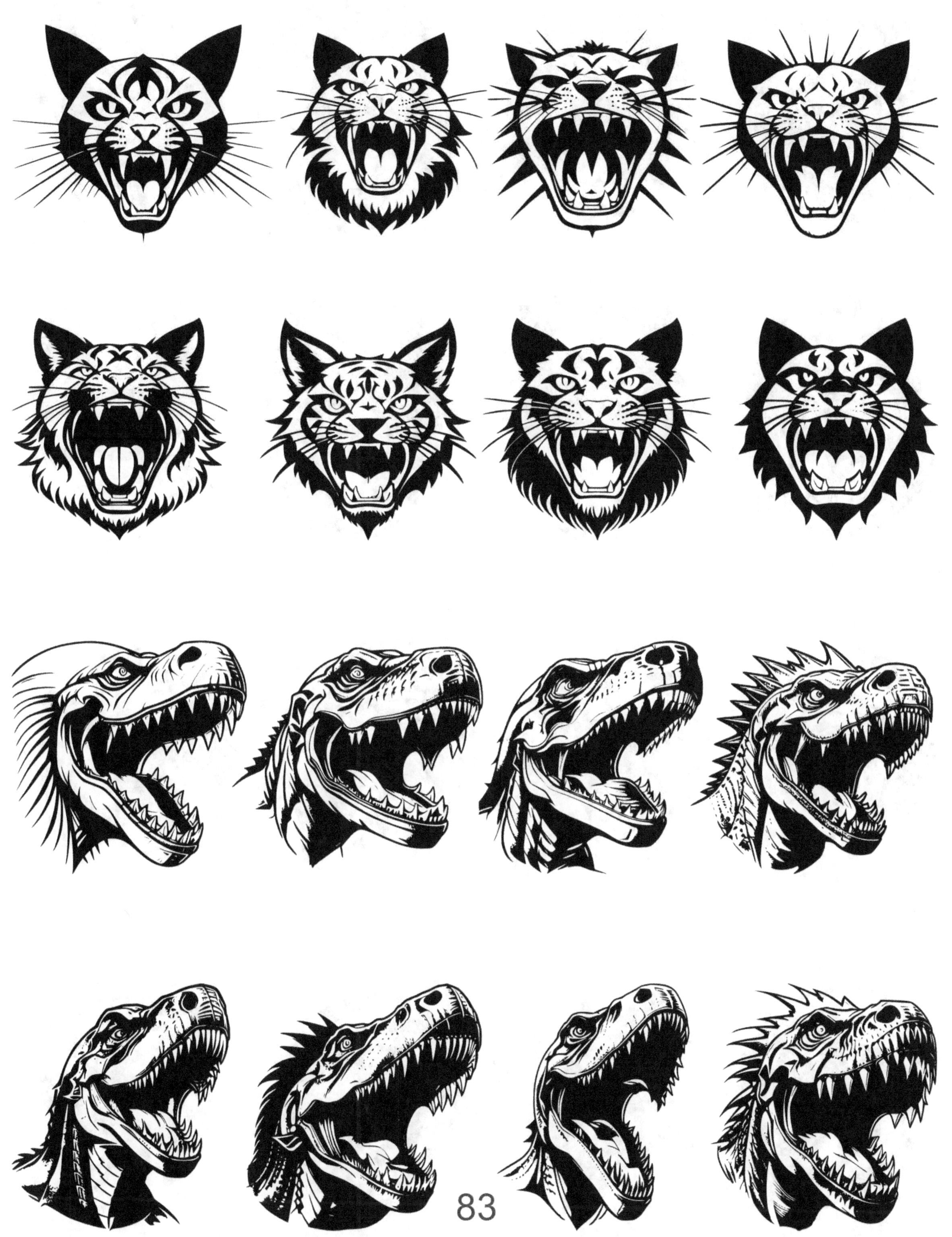

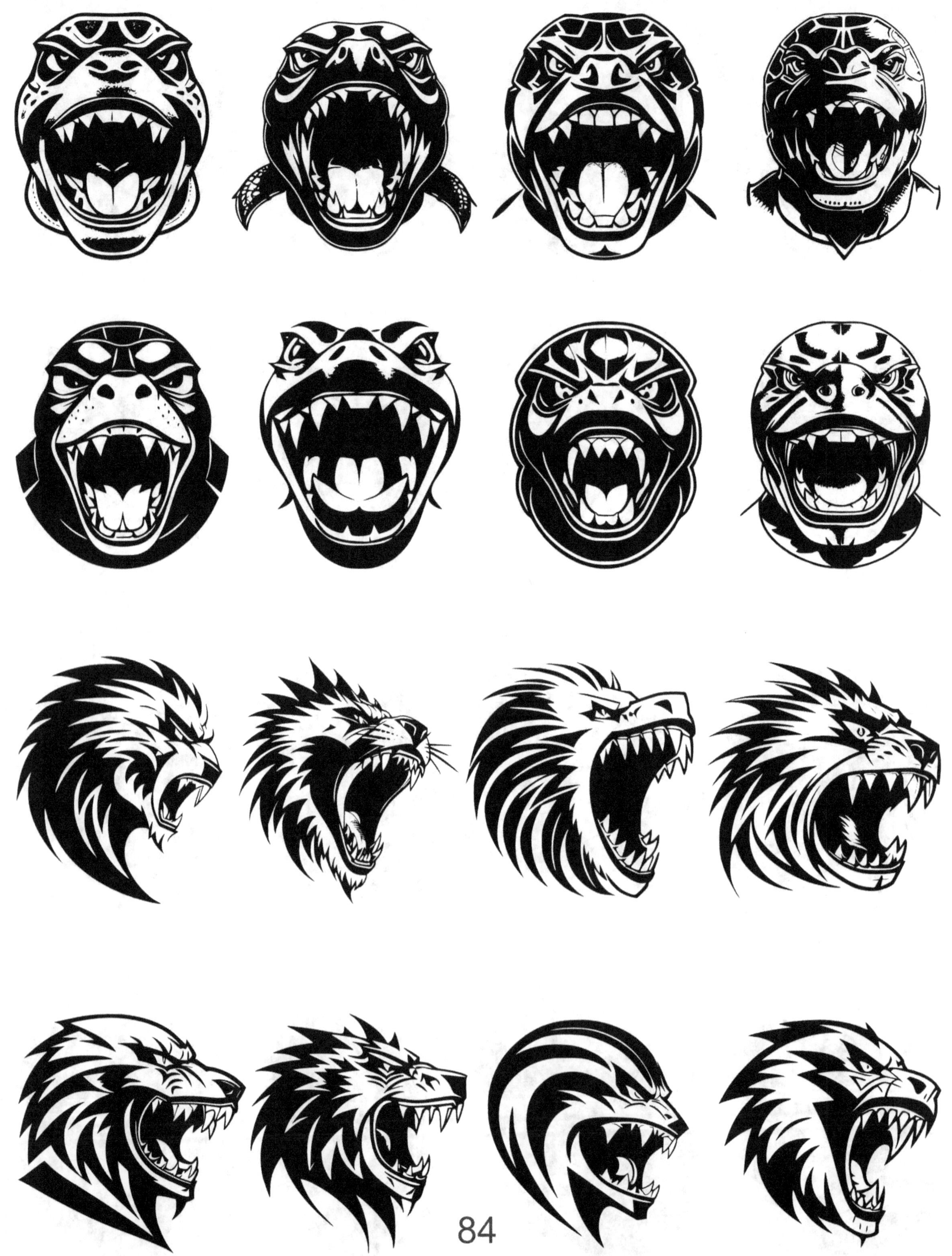

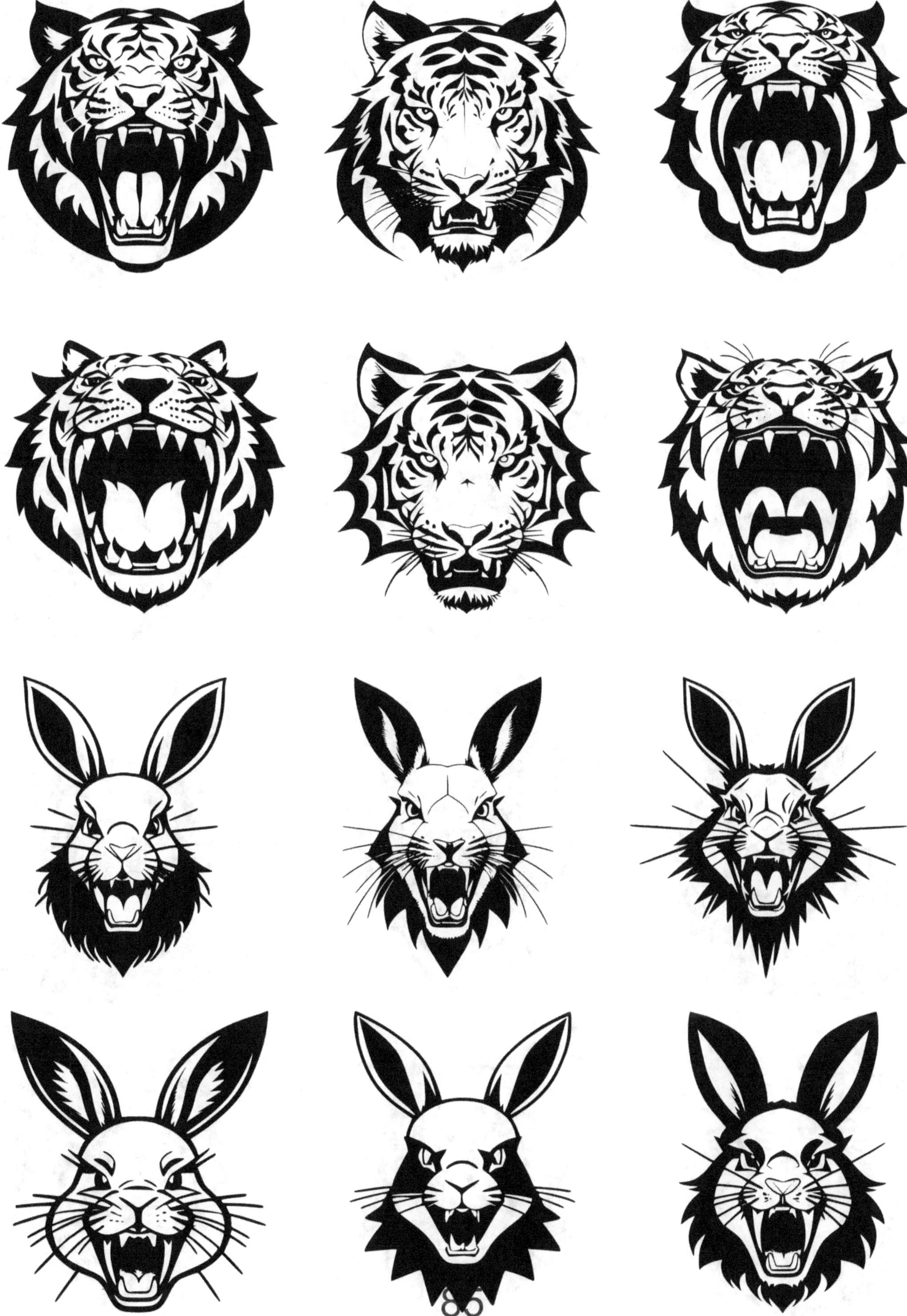

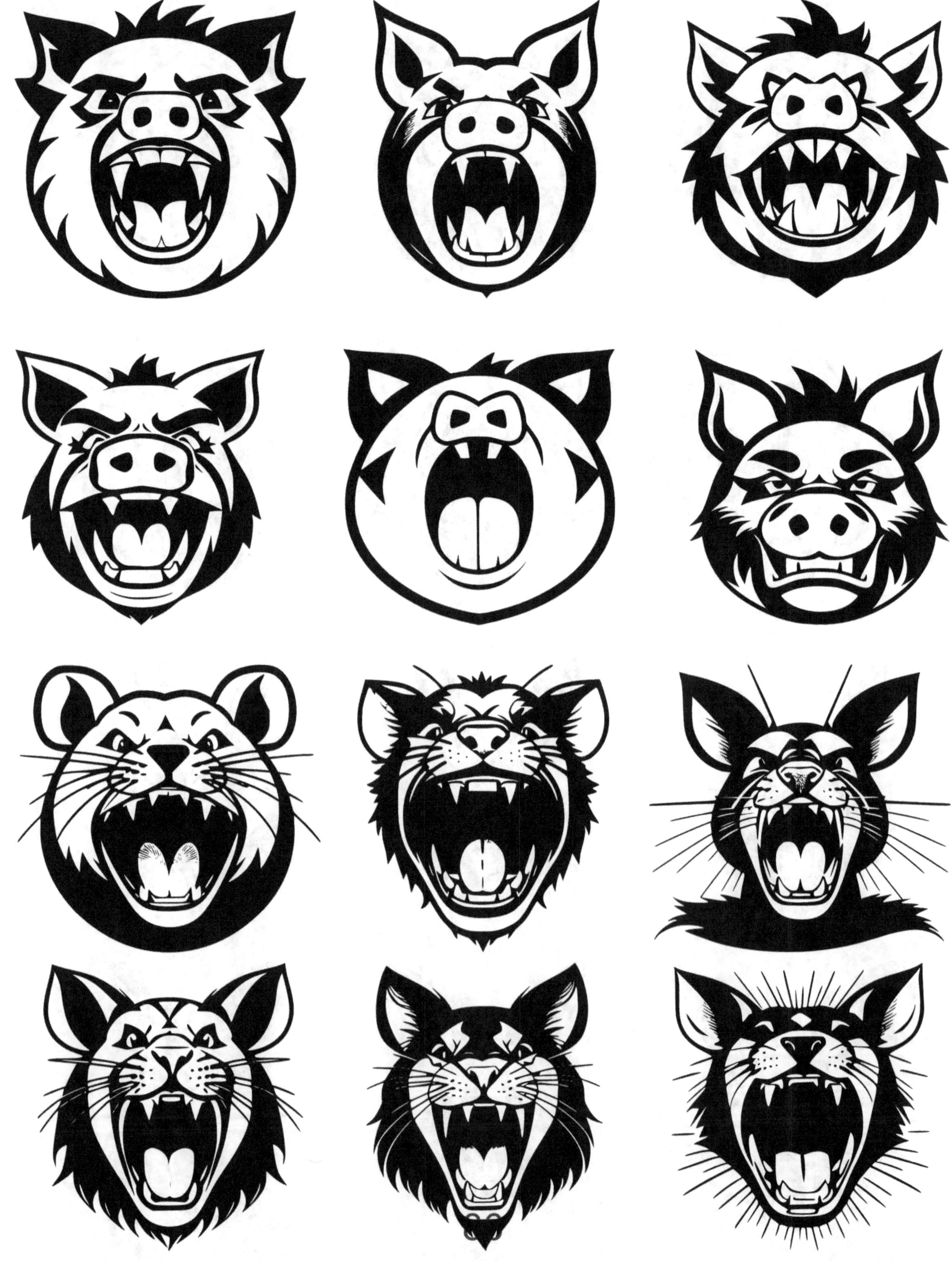

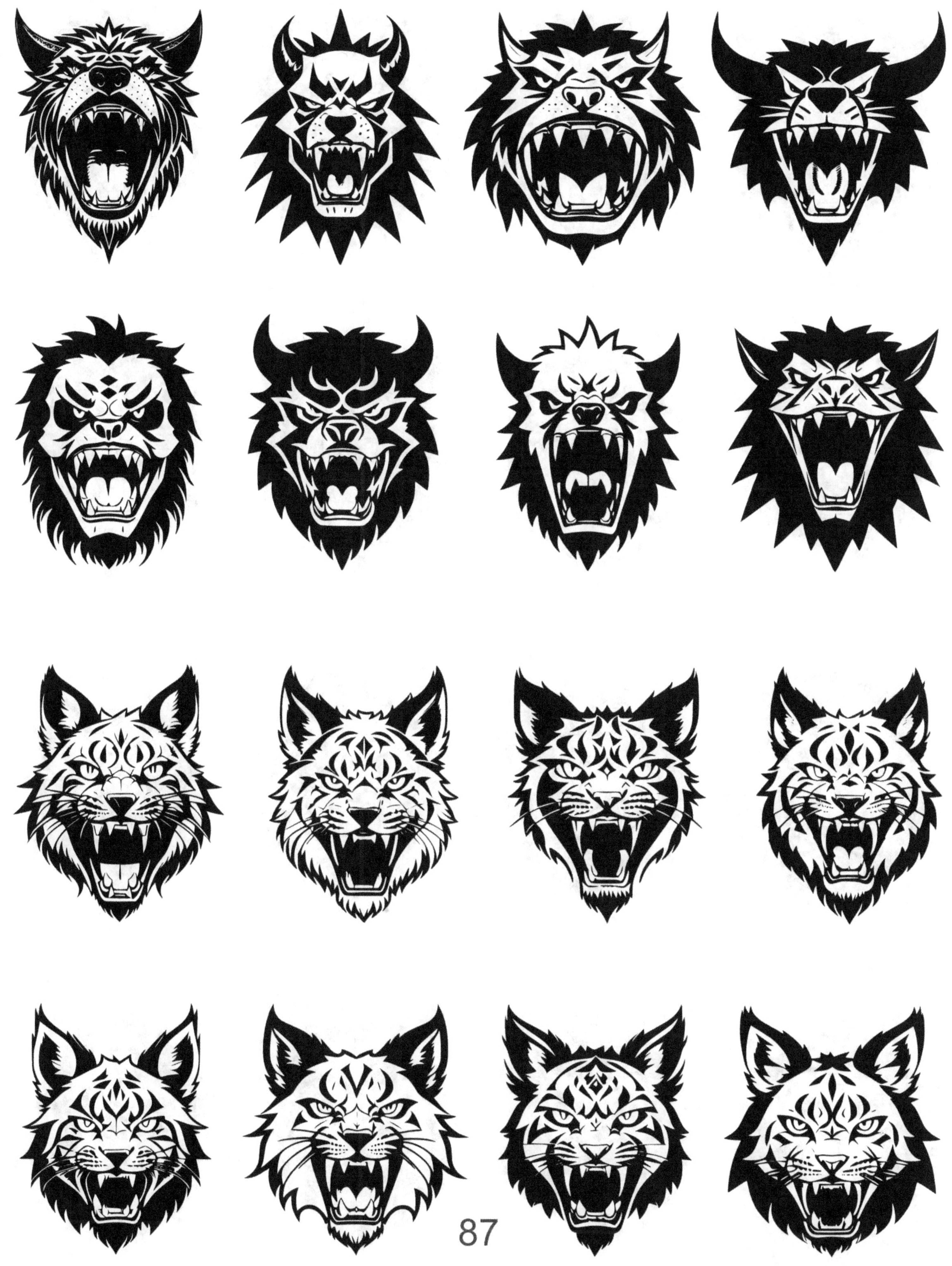

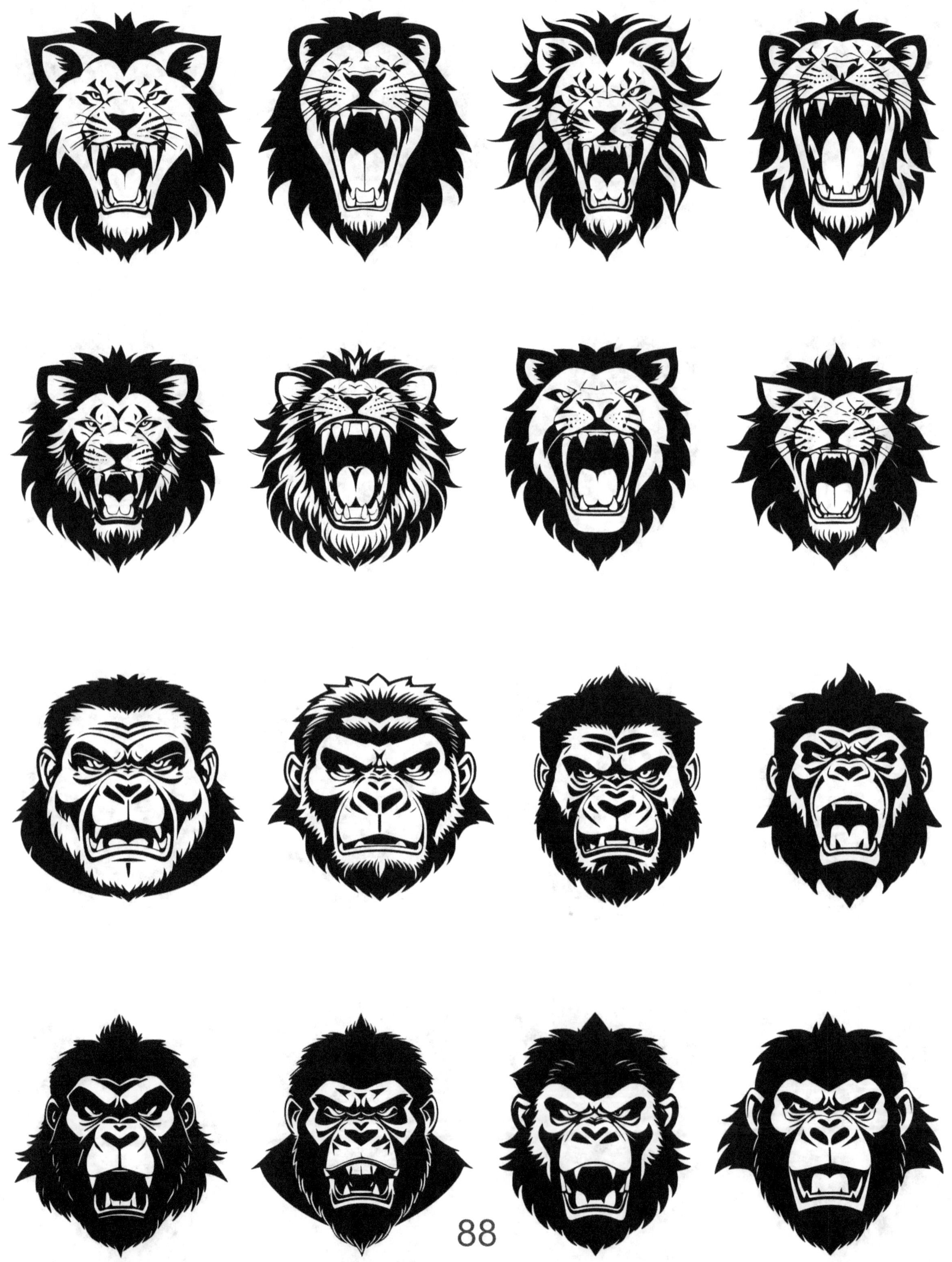

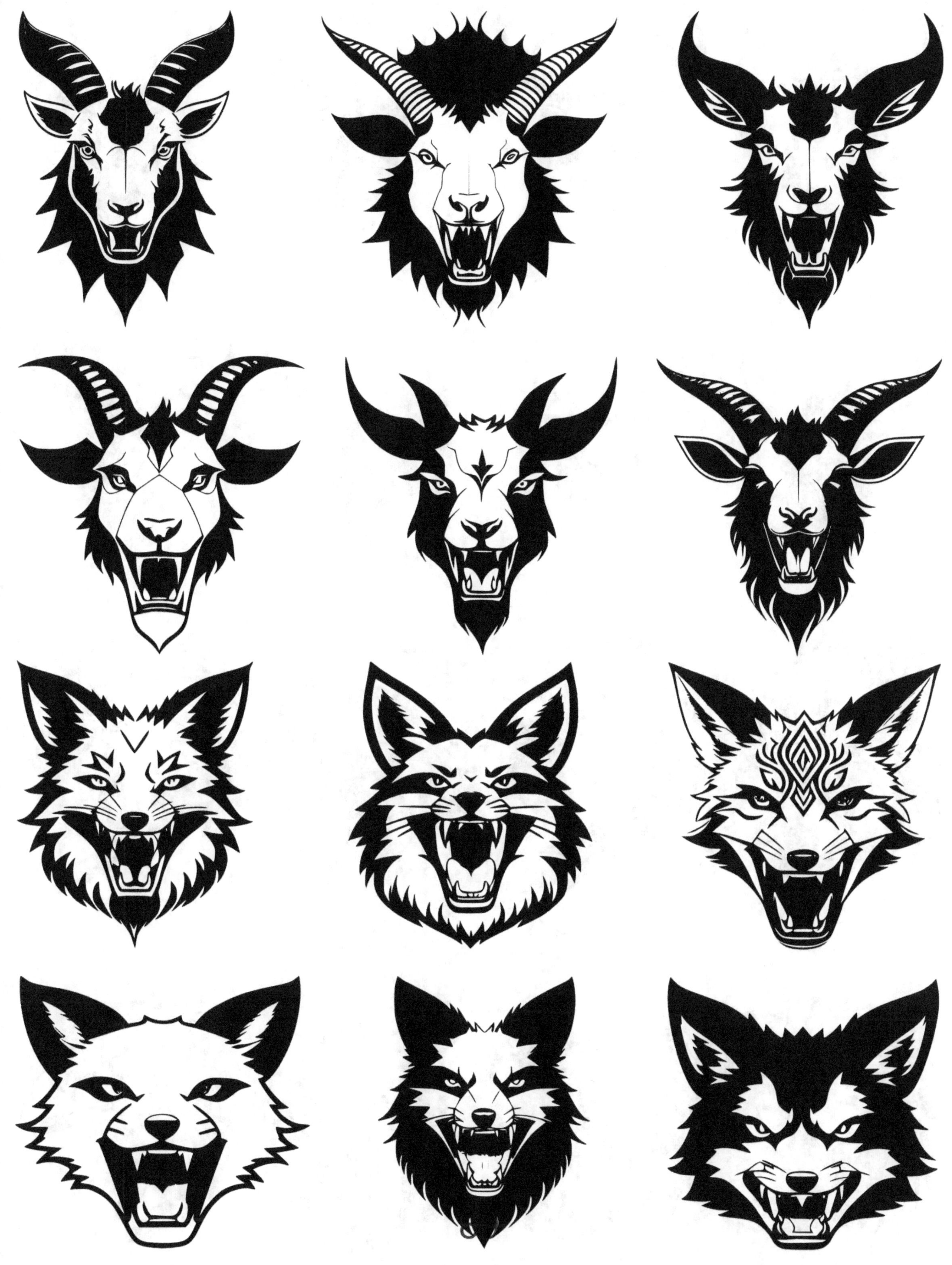

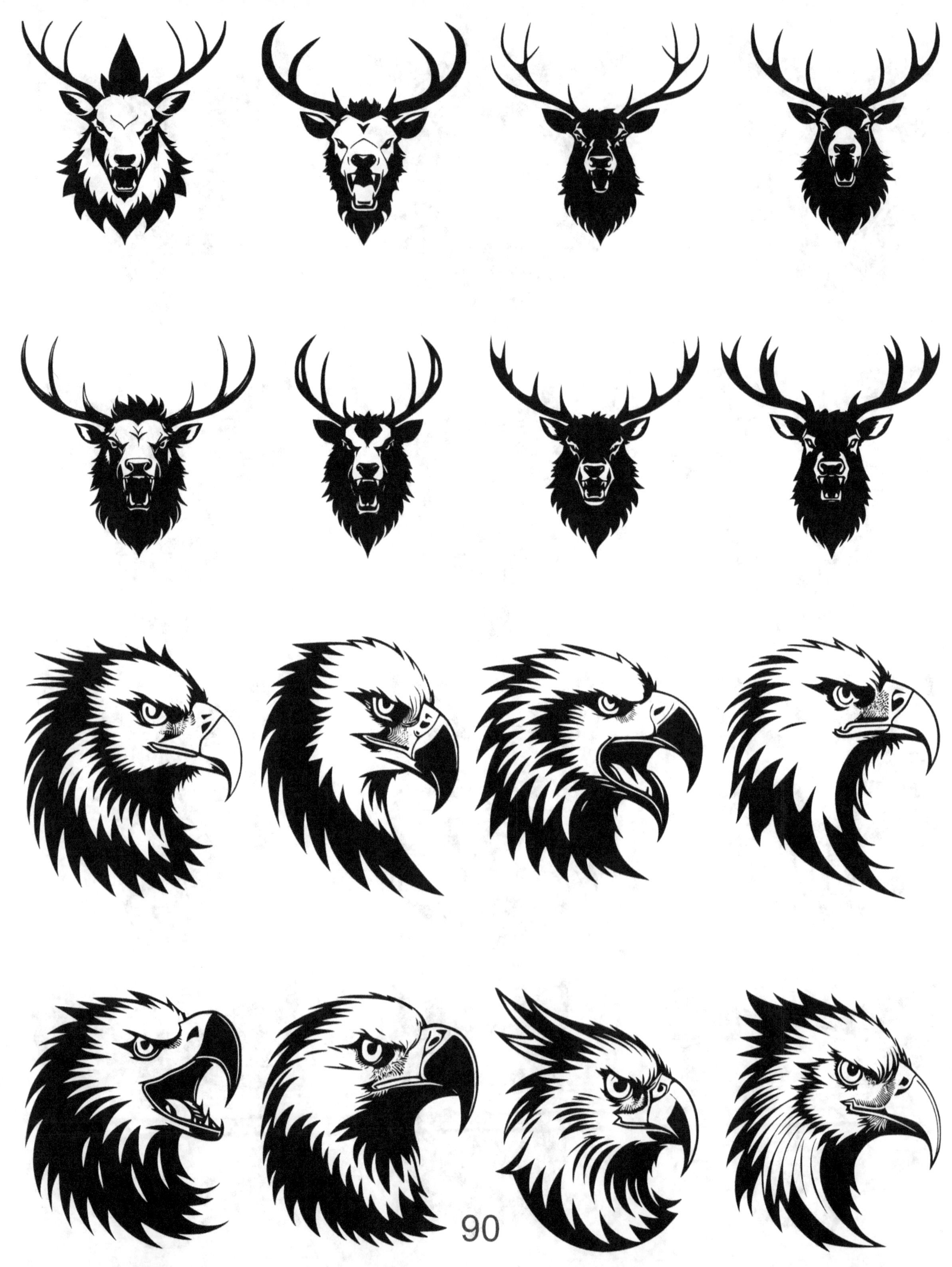

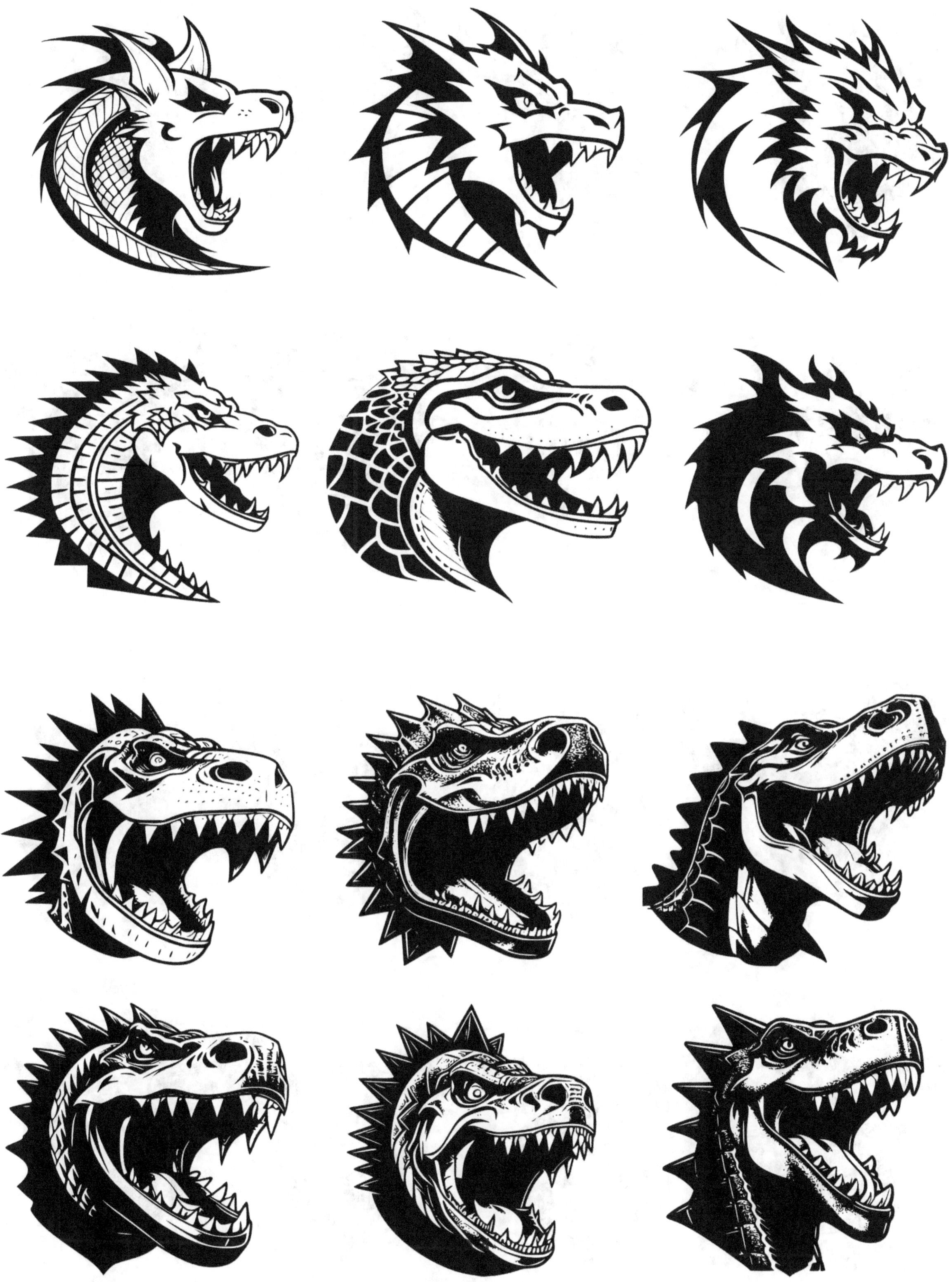

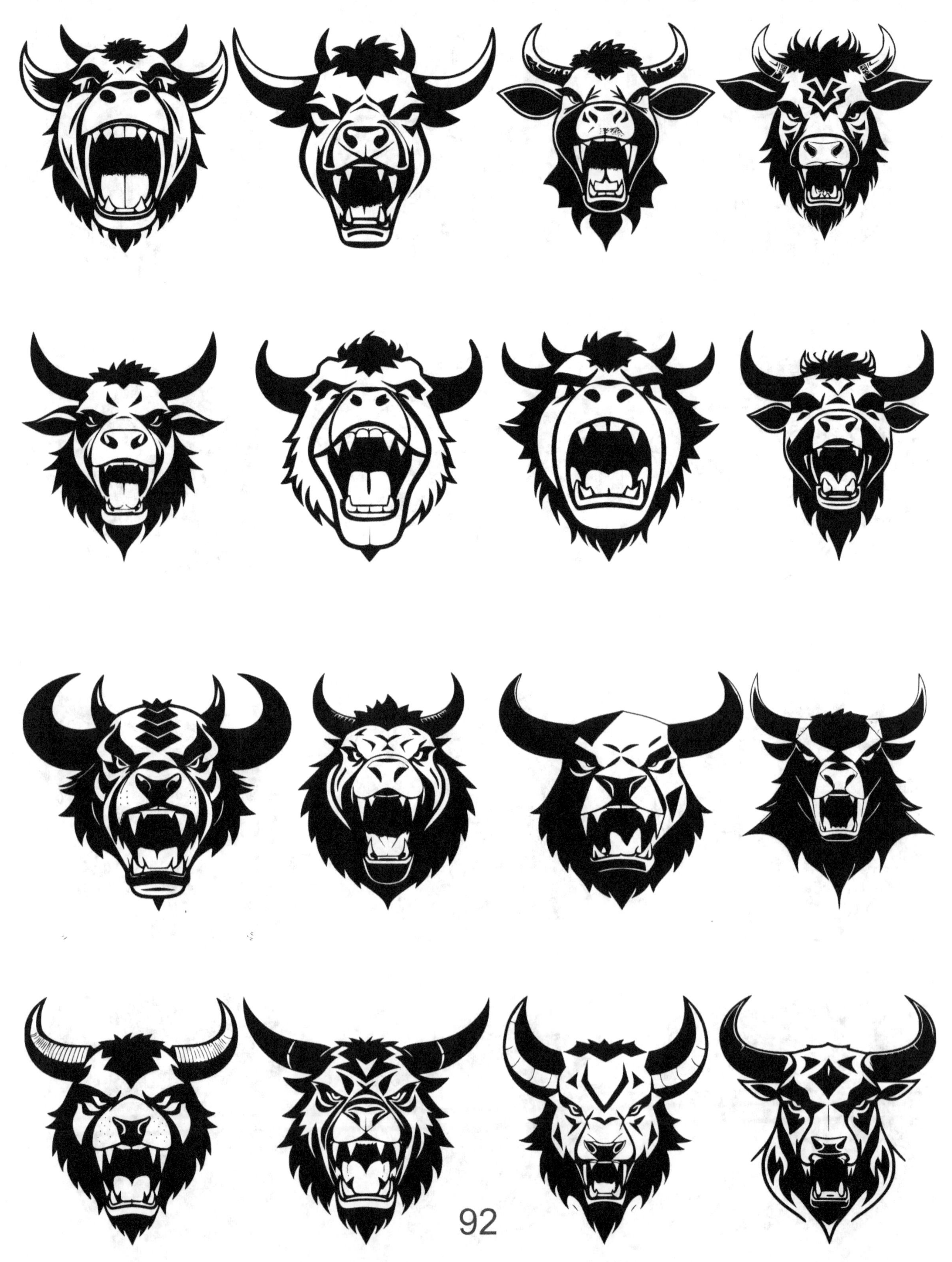

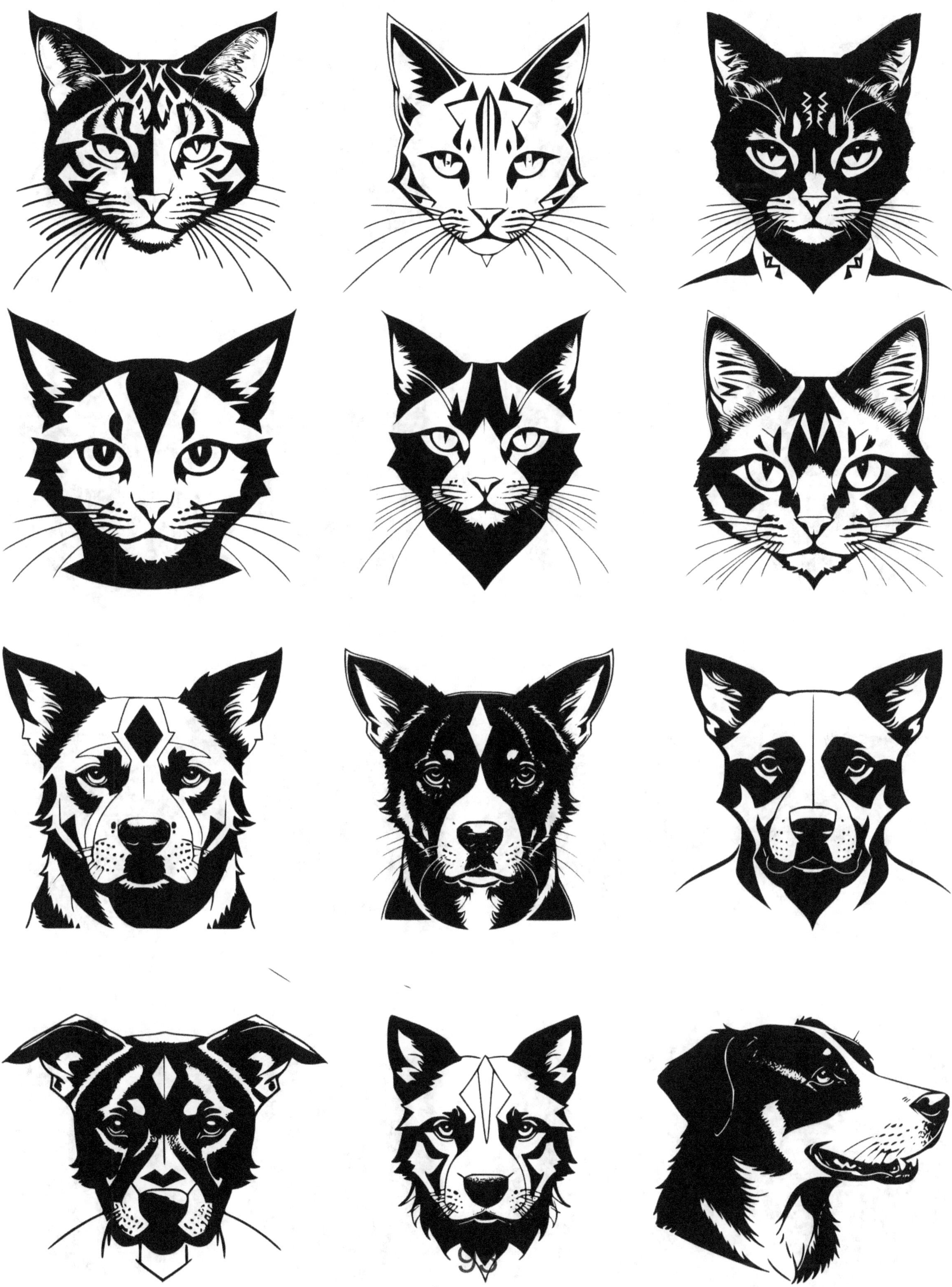

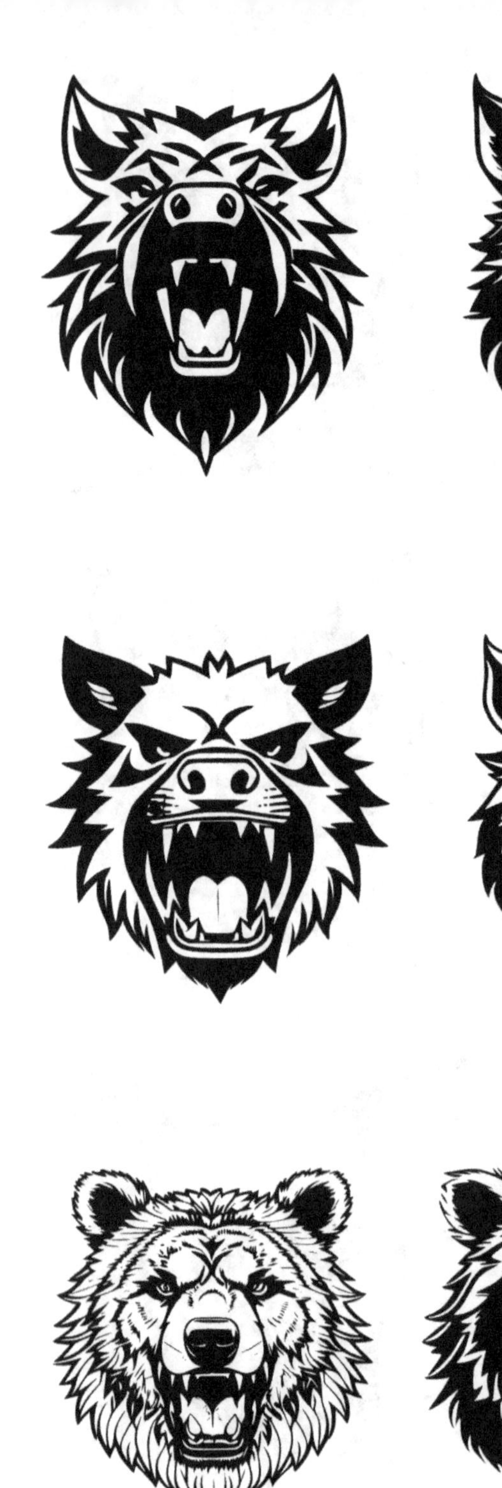
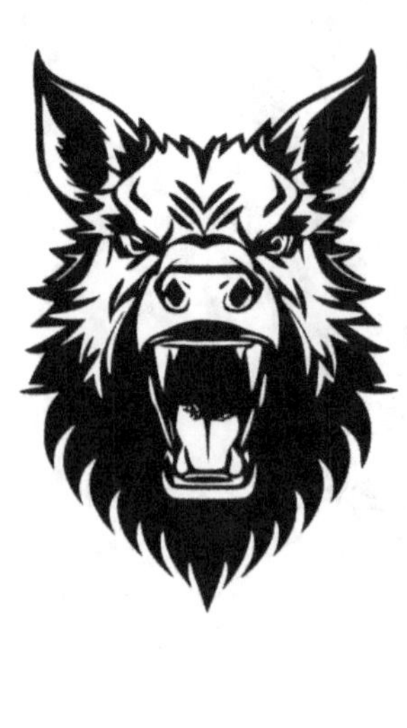
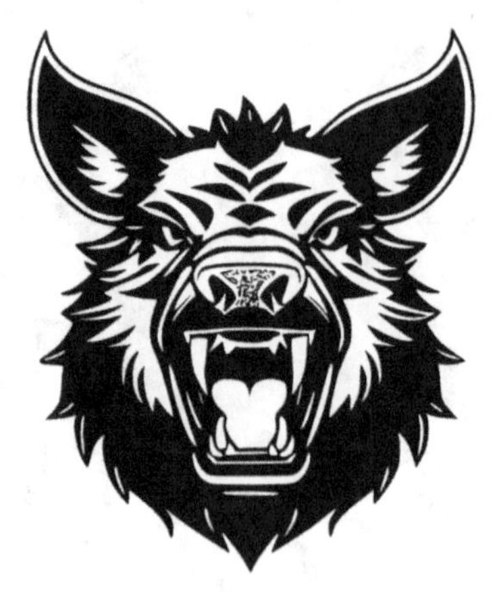
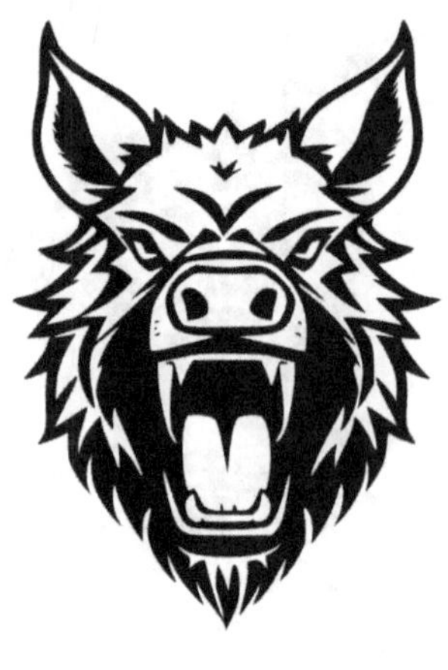
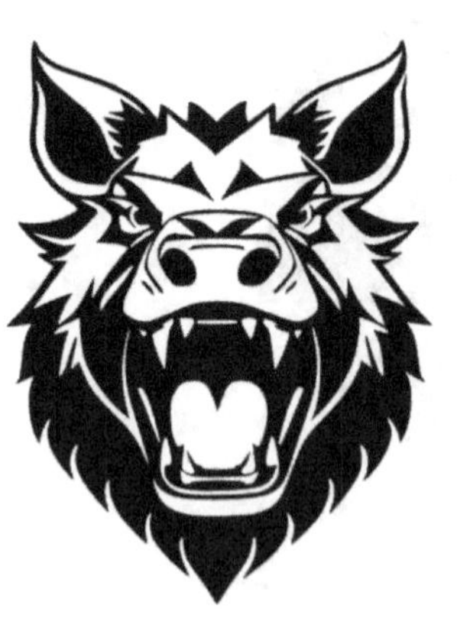
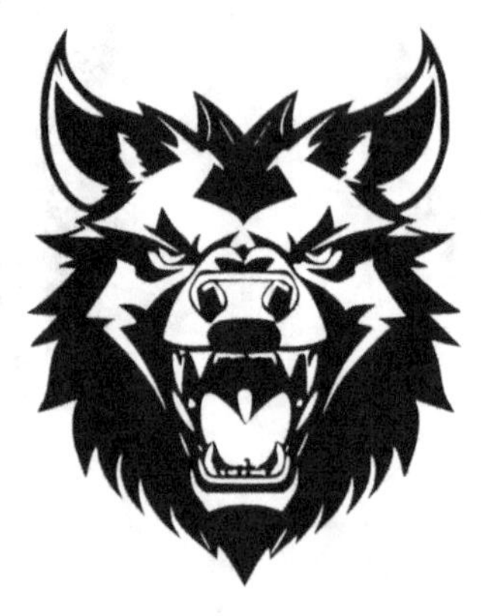
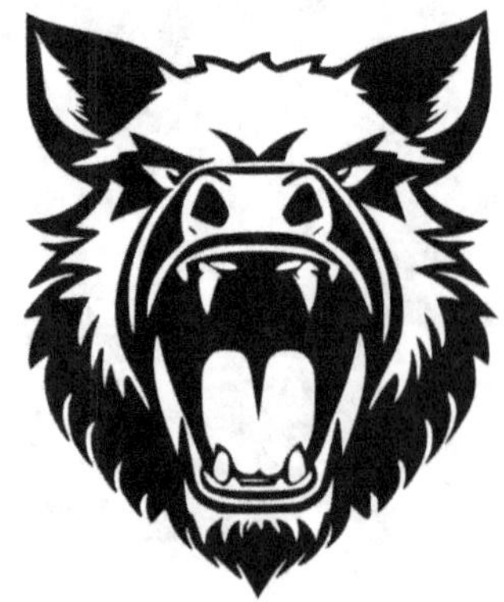
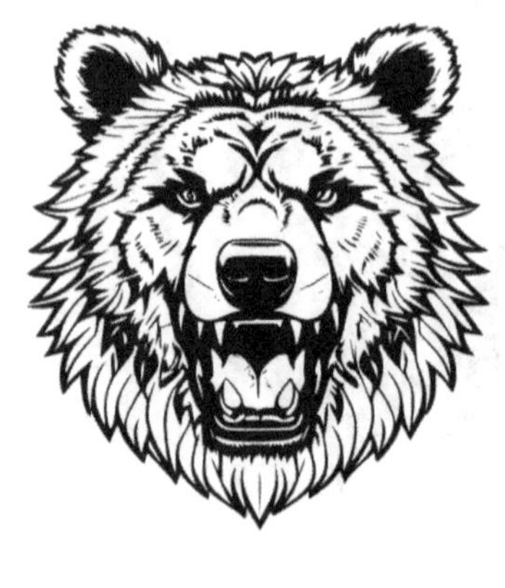
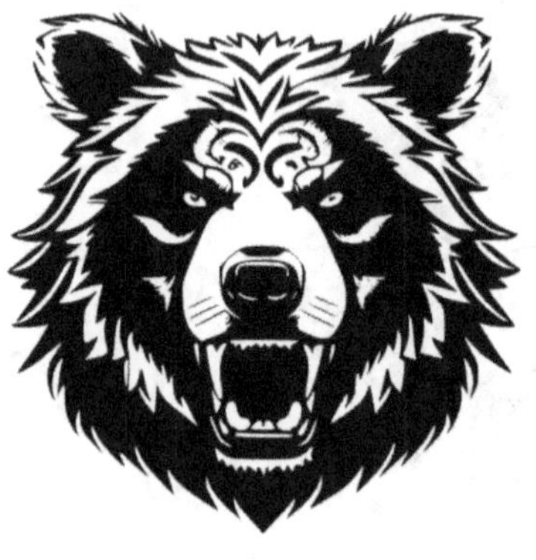
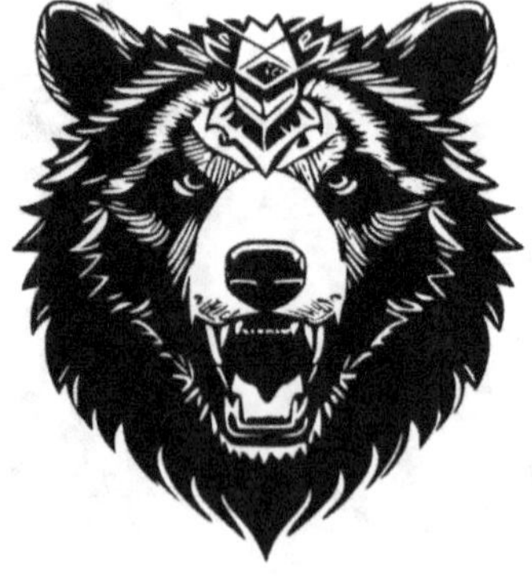
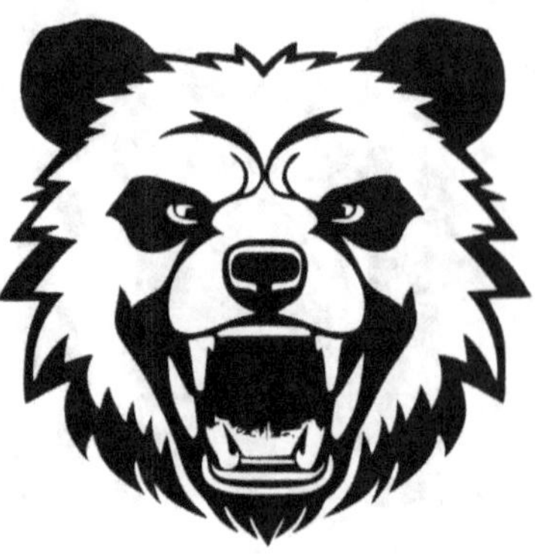
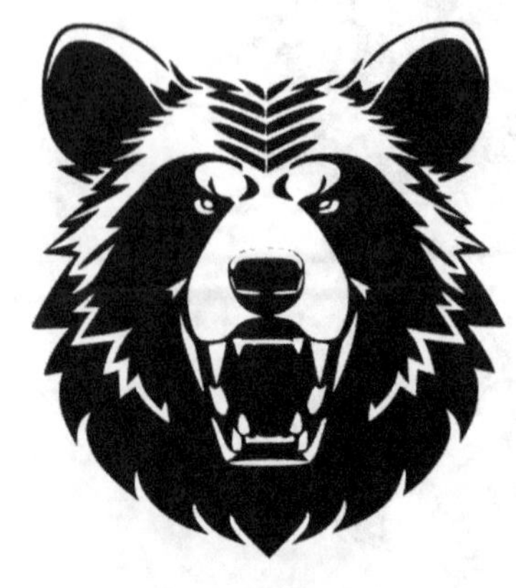
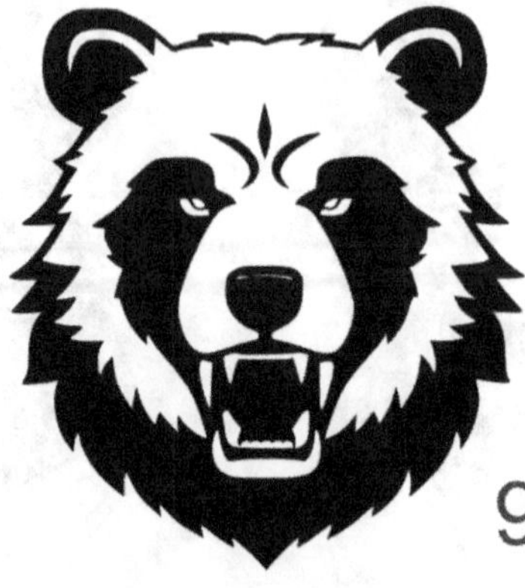
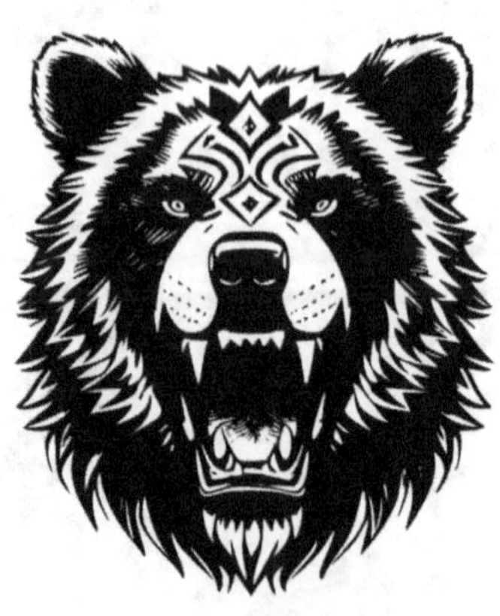
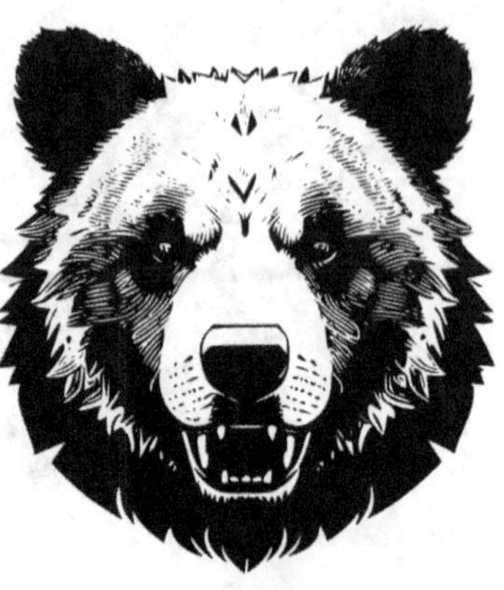

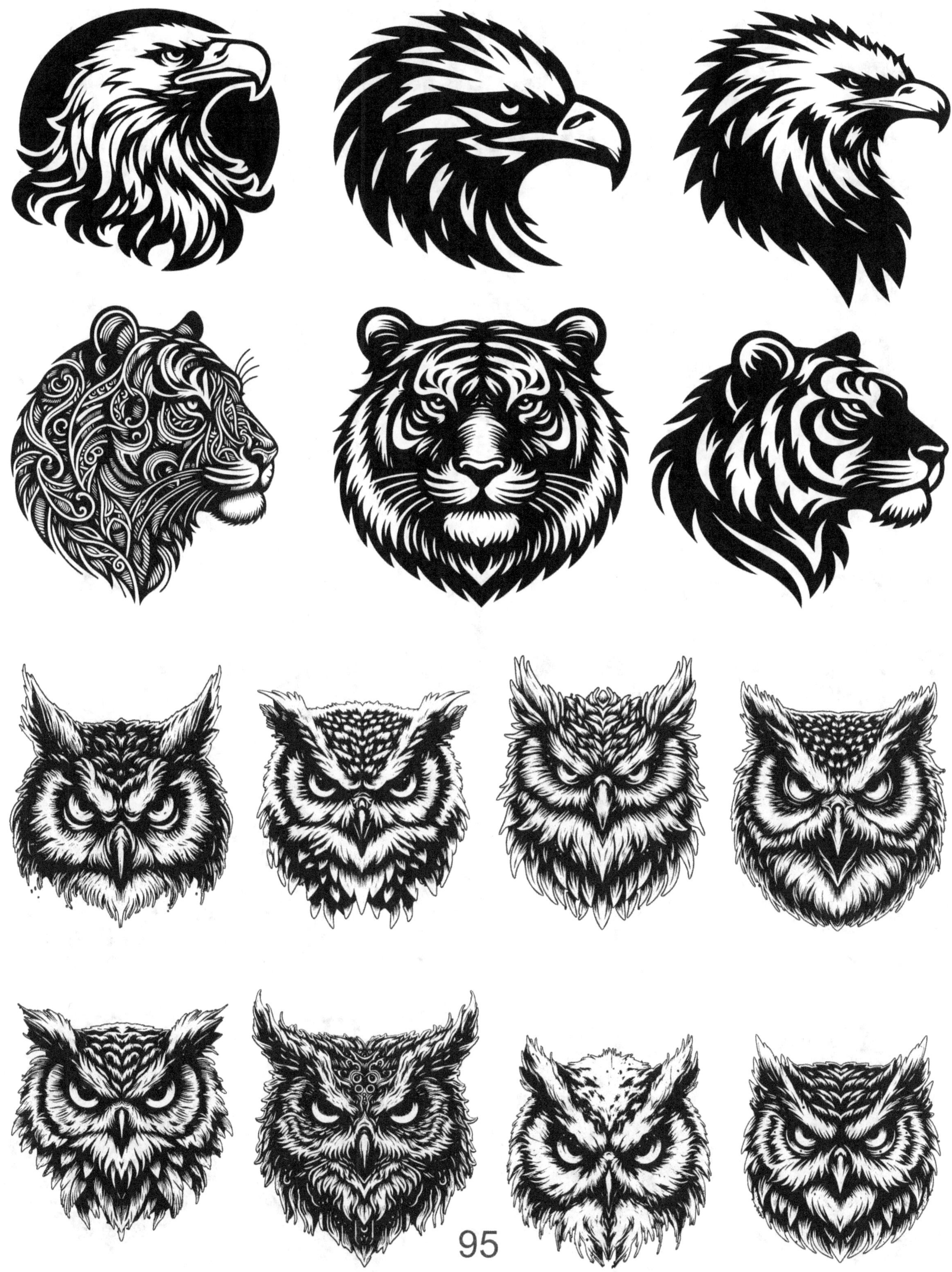

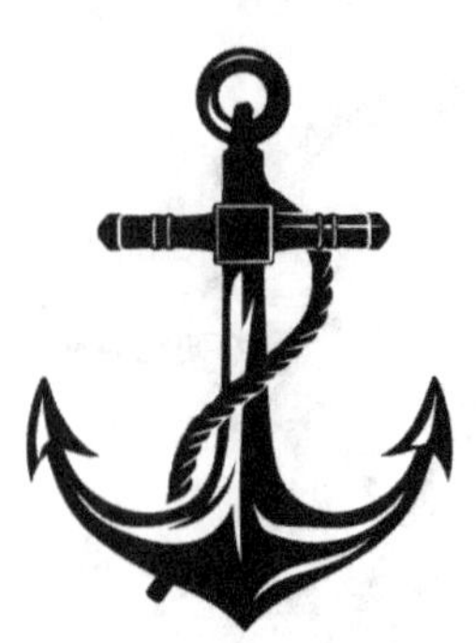
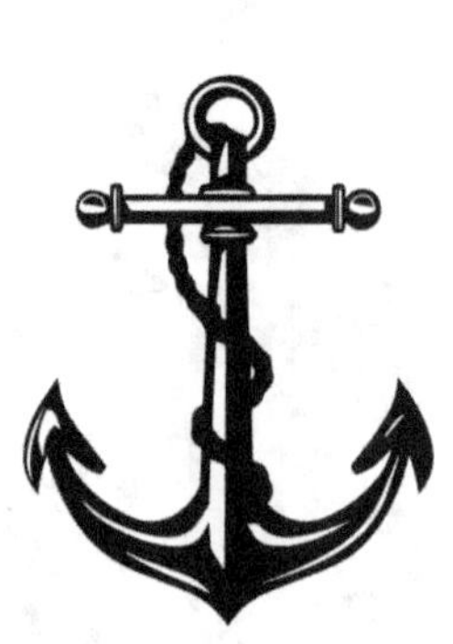

ANCHOR
TATTOOS

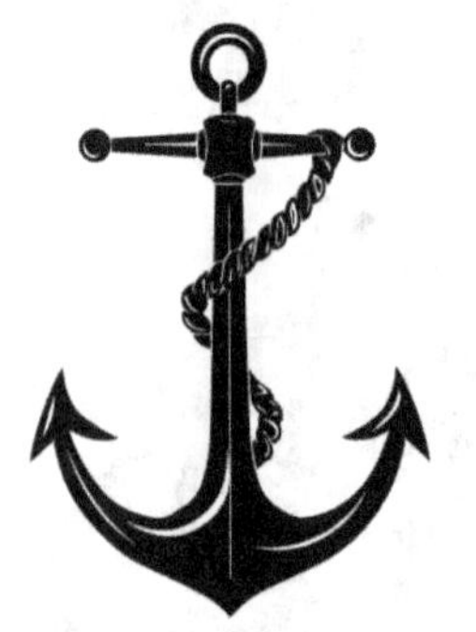
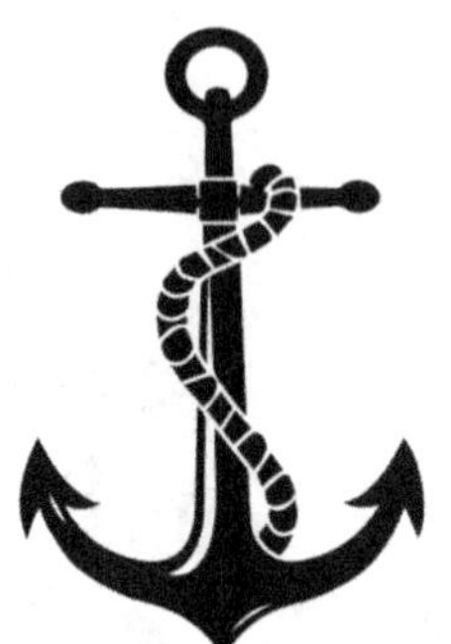
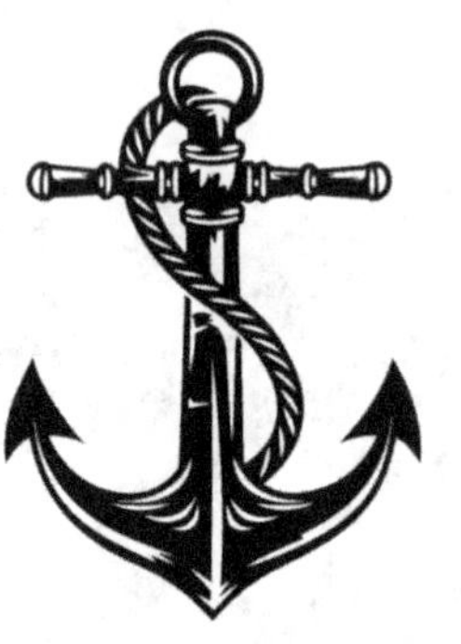
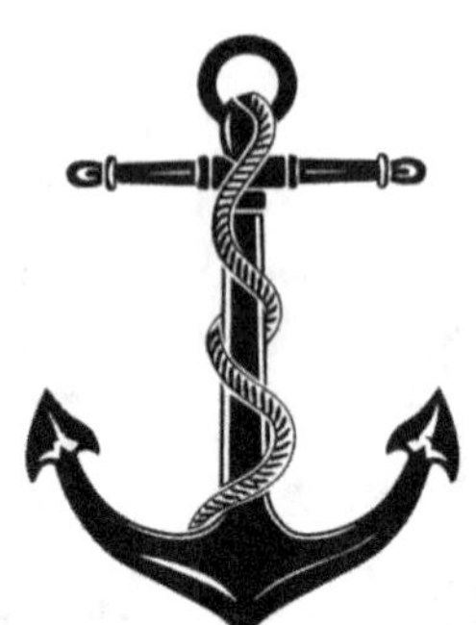
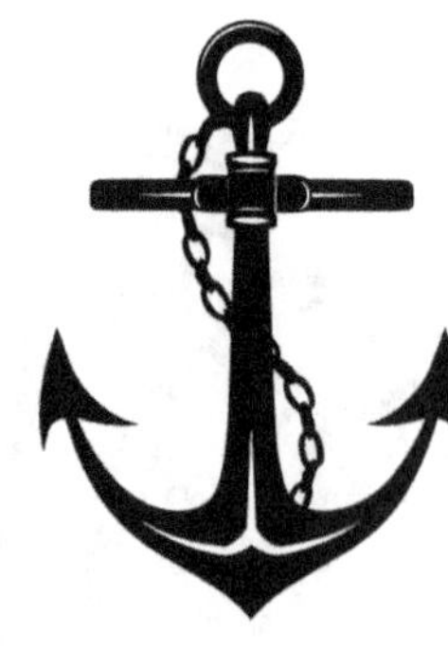

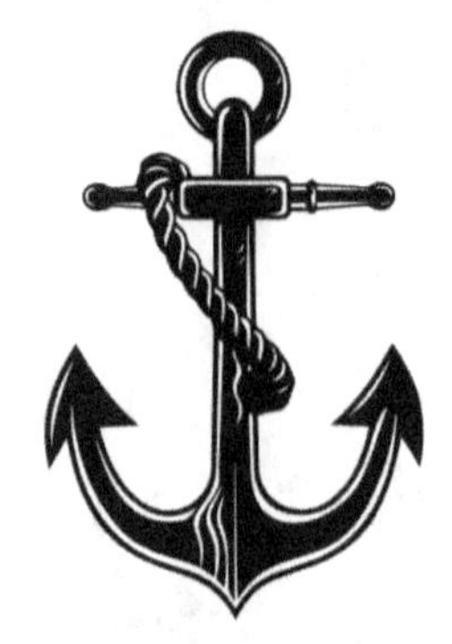
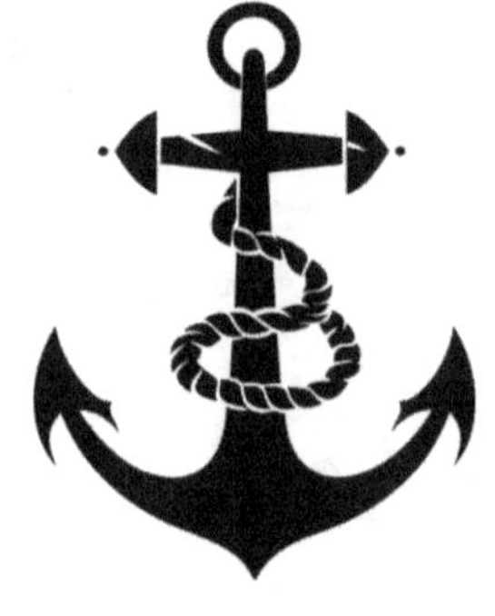

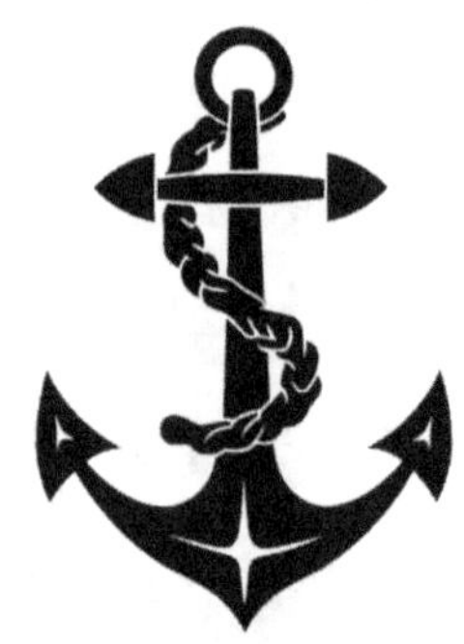
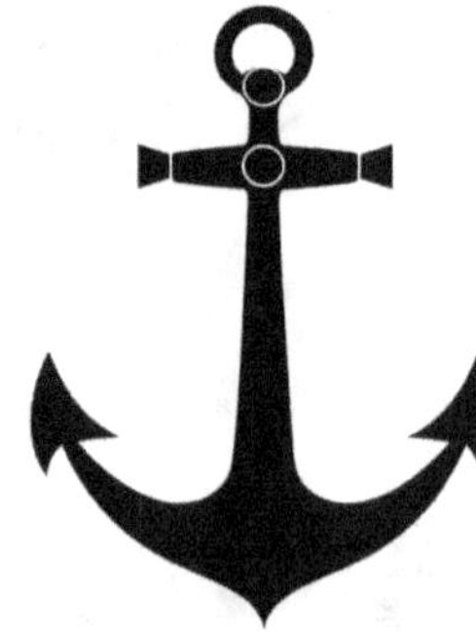

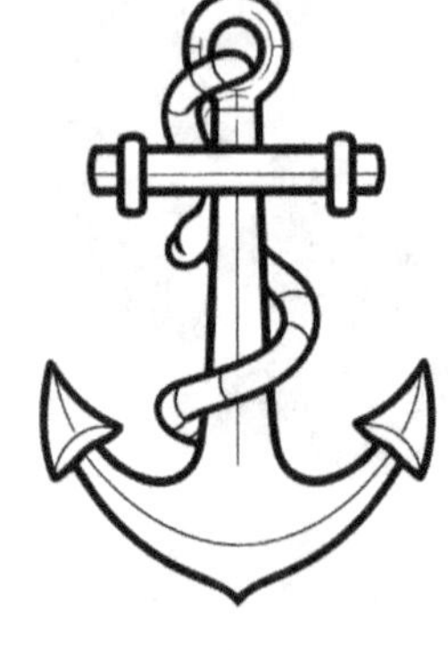
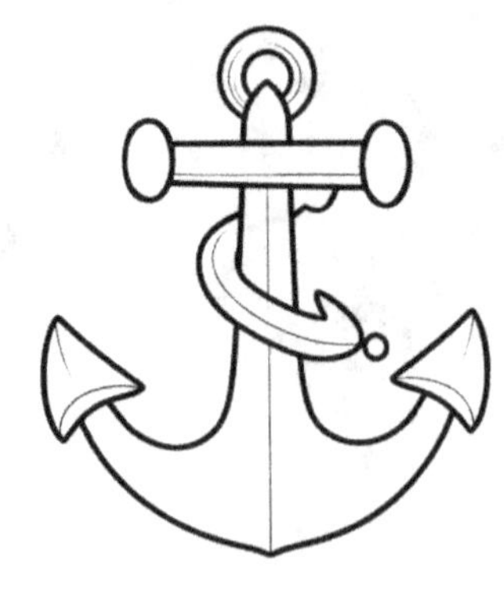
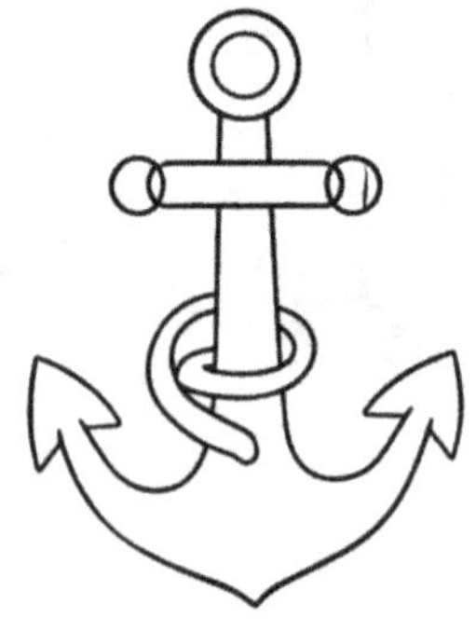

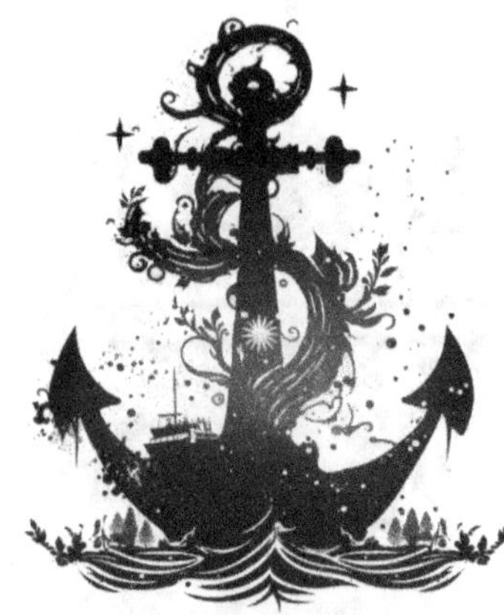
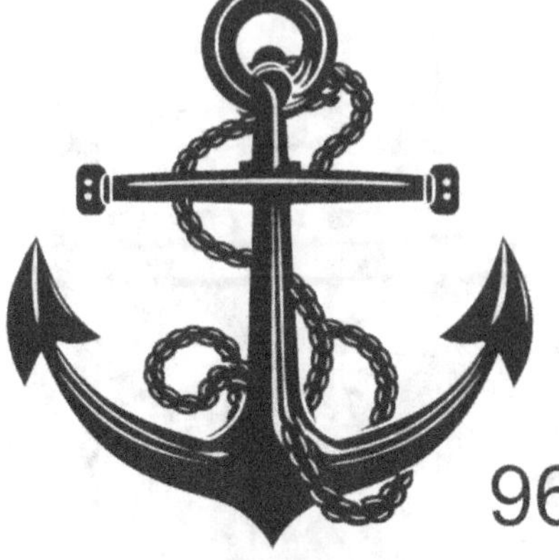
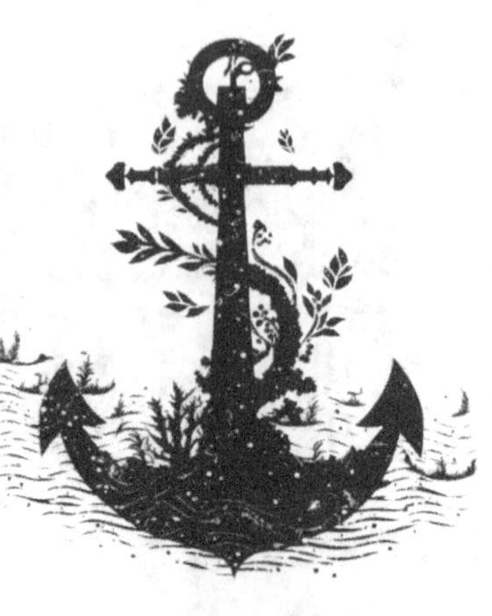
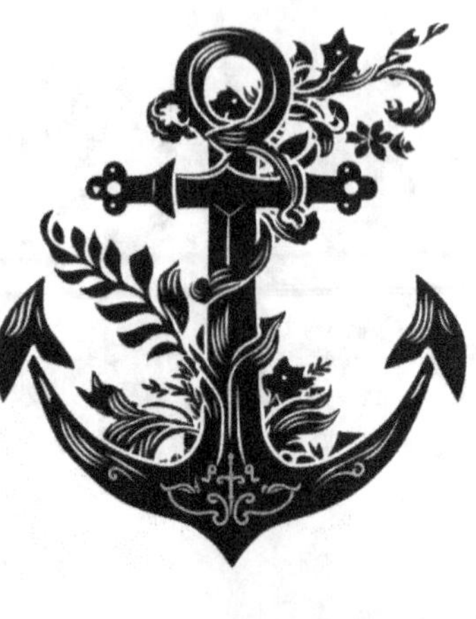

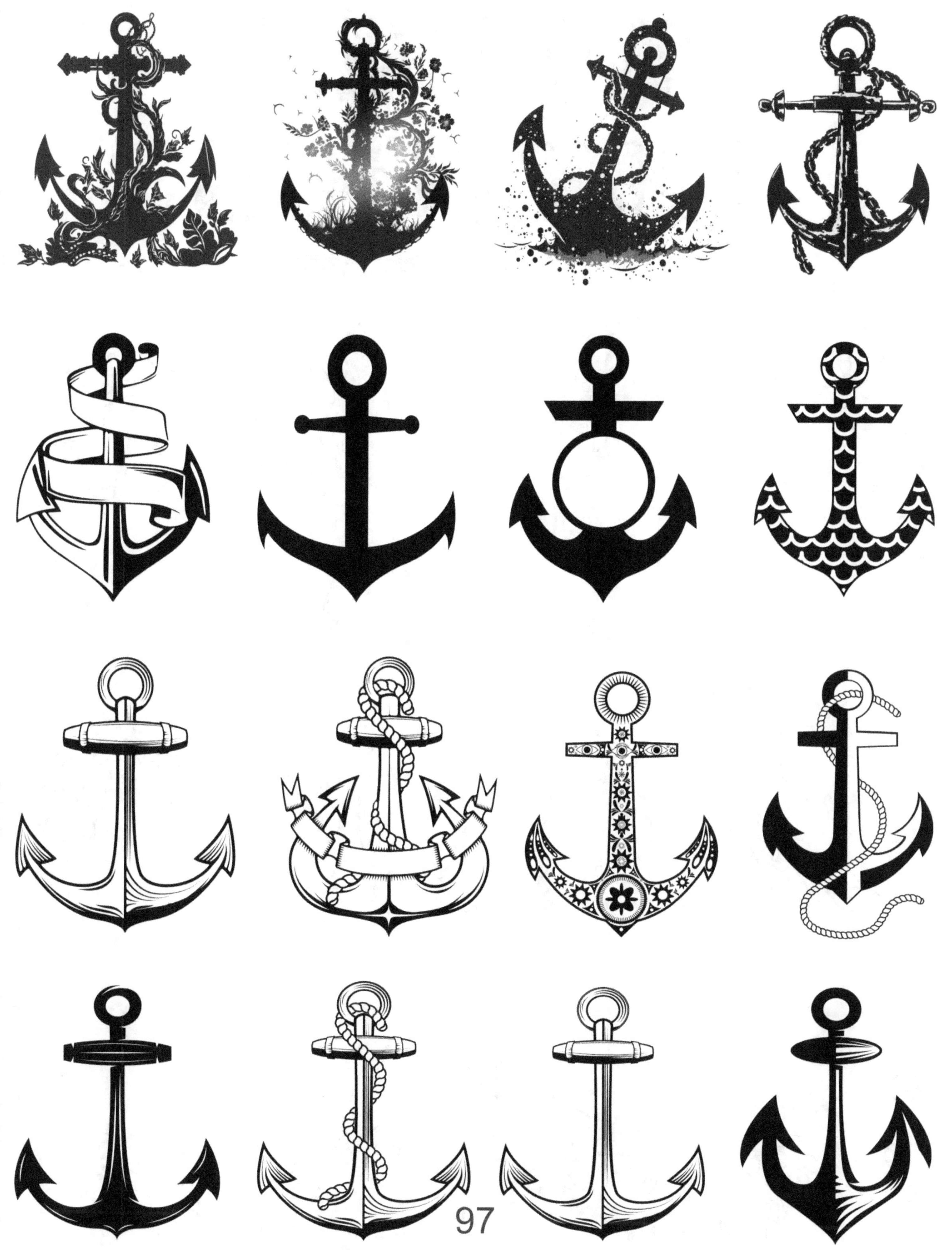

WINGS TATTOOS

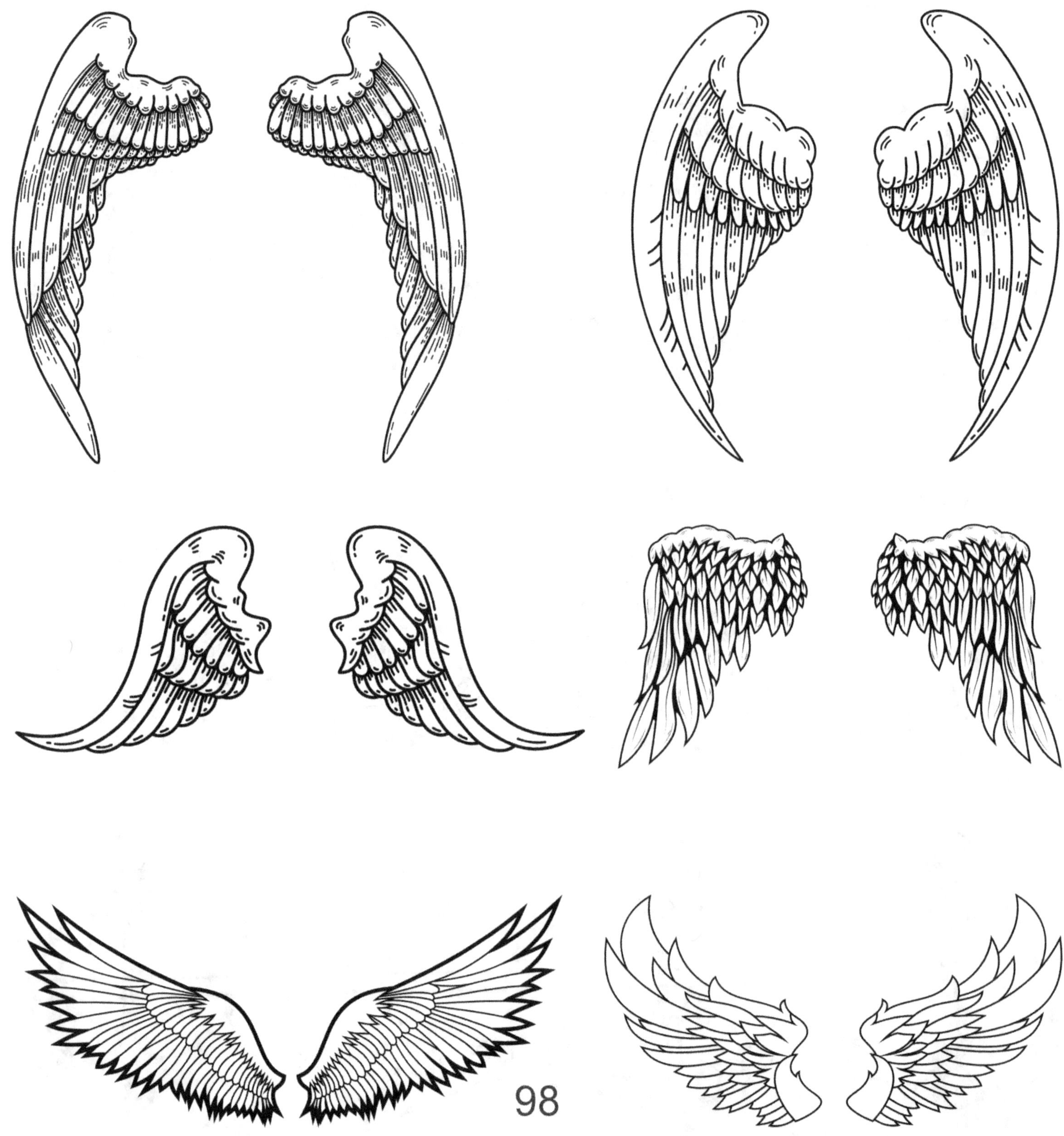

Angel
Angel
angel
Angel

I HOPE YOU ENJOYED EXPLORING THE "TATTOO DESIGN BOOK"! THANK YOU FOR TAKING THIS CREATIVE JOURNEY WITH ME. I'M THRILLED TO HAVE BEEN PART OF YOUR TATTOO ADVENTURE.

TATTOOS ARE MORE THAN JUST ART ON SKIN; THEY ARE POWERFUL EXPRESSIONS OF INDIVIDUALITY, MEMORIES, AND DREAMS. EVERY DESIGN YOU'VE ENCOUNTERED IN THIS BOOK IS A TESTAMENT TO THE LIMITLESS CREATIVITY AND DIVERSE STORIES THAT TATTOOS CAN REPRESENT. I HOPE YOU FOUND INSPIRATION IN THE PAGES AND PERHAPS EVEN DISCOVERED THE PERFECT DESIGN FOR YOUR NEXT TATTOO.

REMEMBER, EACH TATTOO IS A PIECE OF ART THAT TELLS YOUR UNIQUE STORY. WHETHER IT'S A TRIBUTE TO A LOVED ONE, A SYMBOL OF PERSONAL GROWTH, OR AN EXPRESSION OF YOUR PASSIONS, LET IT BE A MARK THAT YOU'RE PROUD TO CARRY.

KEEP CREATING, KEEP DREAMING, AND KEEP TELLING YOUR STORY THROUGH YOUR ART.